Come on, Dad!

75 Things for Fathers and Sons to Do Together

by Ed Avis

Illustrated by Geneviève Després

Lobster Press™

Avis, Ed, 1967-
Come on Dad! 75 Things for Fathers and Sons to Do Together
Text © 2002 Ed Avis
Illustrations © 2002 Geneviève Després

Published by Lobster Press™
1620 Sherbrooke Street West, Suites C & D
Montréal, Québec H3H 1C9
Tel. (514) 904-1100 • Fax (514) 904-1101 • www.lobsterpress.com

Publisher: Alison Fripp
Editor: Alison Fischer
Design & layout: Maria Simpson

Distributed in the United States by: Distributed in Canada by:
Publishers Group West   Raincoast Books
1700 Fourth Street   9050 Shaughnessey Street
Berkeley, CA 94710   Vancouver, BC V6P 6E5

We acknowledge the financial support of the Government of Canada through the Book Publishing Industry Development Program (BPIDP) for our publishing activities.

National Library of Canada Cataloguing in Publication Data

Avis, Ed, 1967-
    Come on, Dad : 75 things for fathers and sons to do together

ISBN 1-894222-72-5

    1. Family recreation--Juvenile literature. 2. Fathers and sons--Juvenile literature. I. Fischer, Alison, 1977- II. Després, Geneviève
III. Title.

GV182.8.A95 2002   j790.1'91   C2002-901029-2

Printed and bound in Canada.

To Pop

INTRODUCTION

Remember when you thought your Dad could do just about anything? He always had cool ideas for fun activities, advice for your problems and answers to your questions. Best of all was the time you spent together because he made you feel like the most important person in the world!

Nurture the special bond between you and your son by enjoying time together in interesting, creative ways. *Come on, Dad! 75 Things for Fathers and Sons to Do Together* serves up plenty of fun-filled activities for the two of you to try out. From building a mini-golf course to playing a homemade board game, the suggestions in this book are designed to challenge, educate and stimulate little minds.

Many of the activities are centered around encouraging your son's creativity, through art projects and crafts. There are also word games, silly science experiments, secret codes to unravel and different culinary creations to make. Most of the activities require few supplies and little planning. I have two sons and know that to have a maximum amount of fun, it's best to keep prep-time to a minimum.

These 75 activities are geared to fathers and sons with a wide range of interests. Whether you do three activities in one day or two in a month, the most important part about using this book is to enjoy the time that you get to spend with each other. There's no doubt you'll make lasting memories that you'll both treasure forever.

Ed Avis

A Note from the Publisher:

As always, please be careful when you and your children participate in the activities listed in this book. The publisher and the author encourage parents to exercise caution and good judgment when engaging in any activity with their children, and neither Lobster Press™ nor the author can be held responsible for any accidents that may occur.

TABLE OF CONTENTS

BATHTUB NAVY

T he navy has called young men to the sea for hundreds of years and your son may some day heed the boatswain's whistle. But while he's still too young to pack his duffle bag, take him on an adventure on the high bathtub.

The trick is to make the bathtub battle a two-part adventure. First, help your son fashion a fleet of armored vessels. Aluminum foil is the perfect material. Cut out rectangular pieces of foil, roughly four inches by two inches. Fold them in half so the four-inch sides touch, then squish in the ends and spread open the top, creating crude little boats. You might need to bunch up a little extra foil for a rudder along the bottom of the boat to keep it steady. Make different sized boats and call them battleships, aircraft carriers, destroyers, cruisers or PT boats. Don't worry about all the stuff above the deck—just concentrate on the hull.

Materials Needed

- Aluminum foil
- Empty shampoo bottles

Once your fleet is complete, fill the tub and commence the sea battle. Empty shampoo bottles filled with water make great cannons. See how much water a ship can hold before it sinks. Demonstrate how waves have destroyed many a powerful ship. What happens when a ship loses its shape and becomes just a ball of foil? Whoosh, straight to a watery grave! Do you or any brothers or forefathers have navy experience? Now's a great time to share some sea stories. Or you can visit your local library together to learn about different types of battle cruisers.

Make it harder: Make your boats bigger, add straw and paper sails and send them afloat in a stream or pond.

② NIGHT ADVENTURE

Night is fascinating to young boys who are usually in bed after dark. An excursion outdoors after the sun sets is a special treat for both you and your son.

Plan your adventure ahead of time by packing a light snack, hot chocolate and a flashlight. Suggest your son put on his pajamas to make the experience more special. Discuss what you'd like to see under the flashlight's beam and then

Materials Needed

• Flashlight

step out into the night.

If your son is very young, just about everything will catch his eye. Start by gazing into the night sky. Try to identify familiar constellations such as the big dipper and Orion's Belt. Examine the moon and see if you can spot any craters. Click on the flashlight and shine it towards the ground. If you live in a damp area, it's likely that night crawlers will be in your path. Crouch down and peer under bushes, into crevices in the sidewalk and near the base of trees for other interesting nocturnal creatures. Don't be surprised if your son wants to hold a few of these creepy crawlies.

Keep your eyes and ears peeled for the sight or sound of bigger animals. You might cross a cat, opossum, squirrel or raccoon as it hunts for its dinner. Enjoy your hot chocolate while you sit and listen to the sounds that are all around you; be it the noises of a busy city street or the chirping of a cricket in the distance. Try to guess where each sound comes from and what type of creature or

thing is making the noise.

When you get back inside, ask your son to draw a picture of all the things he saw on your walk.

Make it harder: If your son is older or particularly adventurous, pick a destination together and let your son lead you there.

③
CAMERA DAY

Children are captivated by photographs, especially if they are in the pictures. But, most cameras are off limits to little hands, so indulge your son's curiosity by declaring a Camera Day.

Pick a warm, sunny day so your tyke can take photos indoors or out. Explain how a camera works, how many pictures he'll be able to take and that he must be a certain distance away for the image to come out well. Then, let your little photographer loose.

It's likely you'll be surprised at what your youngster chooses as subject matter. Suggest items or places to photograph if he asks, but let him

Materials Needed

• Disposable camera

do the actual work. It's a good idea to start around the house if he's never tried taking pictures before. Head outside for more diverse subject matter. Combining Camera Day with another trip (to the zoo, for example) is a good way to make lasting memories.

Once the film is done, visit your local film developer and get them to explain how the negatives get turned into pictures. When you pick up the processed film, sit down and go through them one by one, remembering when and where each photograph was taken. Put them in an album or make a collage from the prints (see page 21).

Make it harder: Teach your son the basics of photo composition before you start your day. Use your camera to take similar pictures as your son and then compare prints when they get developed.

Make it easier: Help your son take the pictures; he decides what to photograph, you take the shot.

PLANT A GARDEN

P laying in the dirt is something all kids enjoy doing, especially when they're not supposed to. Turn this habit into a positive, structured activity by designing and creating a garden together.

Even if you live in an apartment complex in the middle of a big city, gardening is still possible. And many suburbs offer plots for rent for a minimal fee. The first thing to do, once you've picked a spot in your garden (or purchased flower boxes), is to decide what to grow. As most gardeners will tell you, it's a smart idea to start off small, choosing three or four types of plants for your first year. Certain plants, such as squash, radishes, tomatoes and carrots grow well under amateur care. Many flowers (Chrysanthemums and Gerbera Daisies, for example) require very little care and are especially pleasant in window gardens.

Once you've decided on the crops, make sure the place you've chosen for your garden has adequate sunlight. The seed packets you purchase at the hardware store will tell you how much light each plant requires.

Don't make your plot much bigger

Materials Needed

- Shovel
- Seeds
- Plot of earth or some flower boxes

than four feet by four feet. That should be challenge enough for your little farmer. Let your son wield the shovel or spade to break the earth. Work together to remove the grass from your plot. Drive the shovel about six inches deep all along the border of your garden. Then pop up chunks of sod by  forcing your shovel into the earth at an angle from the border. As you lift each clump up, shake the dirt back into the garden.

The best part for most kids is tilling the soil. You can use a shovel to break up clumps of dirt, or you can do it with your hands, which is much more fun. Eventually you'll end up with a plot of smooth, soft soil. Read the directions on the seed packets carefully before planting. Keep things well spread out in neat rows.

Growing a garden teaches children patience and responsibility. Visit the garden each day together to complete the many tasks that come along with growing plants; watering, weeding and thinning. When the flowers bloom or your crops are ready, take pictures to preserve a memory of your son's accomplishment. Then clean them off and enjoy the fruits of your labor!

⑤
FAMILY TRIVIA GAME

Boys love showing off their knowledge, so creating a Family Trivia Game plays right into their hands. Although it works best with more than two people, you'll still enjoy it if only you and your son are involved.

Start by giving each player, including yourself, some note cards. Each of you should write down a question about your family on one side of each card, and the answer on the other. If your son isn't old enough to write, let him draw a picture of his question. If he's stumped, throw out a few starters for him; what color are Mom's eyes? Who's the oldest person in the family? Where do we keep the dog's collar and leash?

Once the questions are done, the fun begins. If there are only two of you, take turns asking each other questions. If there are more players, everyone takes a turn at being the

Materials Needed

• Note cards or other small pieces of paper
• Pen

"contestant." They can request a question from anyone who is playing the game. Each correct answer earns 500 points. Keep a tally to see who knows the most about your family. Hints are allowed and you can take up to three guesses for tough questions. When you've finished, put all the cards in a shoe box and store it away for another day.

Make it harder: Expand the trivia to include relatives, neighbors or friends.

6

PERSONAL PIZZAS

Although most families have ordered pizza for delivery at one time or another, kids thrill to make their own. It's the ultimate junk food and great for a snack or meal, so you can do this activity anytime.

Start by checking what is in the fridge. Pre-made crusts or flat breads make preparing this dish a snap. Once you've smeared your crust with sauce, let your kids add whatever toppings they like best. Don't have the standard pepperoni, mushrooms and green peppers? No problem. Try a taco-style pizza with refried beans and spicy ground beef. Use sliced hot dogs, bologna or salami instead of pepperoni and canned corn, peas, and sliced tomatoes. Don't forget to cover the top with cheese, then put it in the oven until the cheese is lightly browned (400 °F for 7 to 15 minutes depending on toppings).

It's a good idea to chop up veggies, shred cheese, cook ground beef or hot dogs before you start so your son doesn't spend hours playing with his food. Pizza is a simple treat that your kid will love, especially since he made it himself. While you are waiting for it to cook, ask your son to help you

clean up the mess so there'll be nothing to do but enjoy the pizza when the timer rings.

Make it harder: If you're ambitious, make the crust by hand. Recipes vary, but the basic ingredients are flour, yeast and water. Or, make a dessert pizza and pile the crust with sweets such as chocolate chips, licorice and other junk food you have hanging around.

⑦
PHOTO COLLAGE

Most households have boxes of unsorted photographs stuffed into closets. They're reminders of family events, birthday parties, sporting activities and dress up days. Most of these pictures, however, are quickly filed or put away after being processed and are rarely seen again.

When you do haul out the photos to look for something specific or reminisce, kids enjoy peering over your shoulder and hearing the stories about each one. To give your son a chance to do something creative and fun, the next time you pull out those pictures, make a

Materials Needed
- Photographs
- Scissors
- Poster board
- Picture frame
- Tape

photo collage with them.

First, clear a table or large floor space to work on. Then, spread a sheet of poster paper or some other sturdy backing material on your hard surface. If you plan to create a more elaborate project by framing the collage, cut the paper to the size of the frame. Then, pile the pictures in the middle of your work space. Encourage your son to paw through the stack and choose photographs that catch his eye.

Let him use kid-friendly scissors to cut out the interesting parts of the picture. As he snips, lay the recently re-shaped photos on the poster board. It doesn't take a professional artist to make a nice layout. Just try to cover the whole backing with pieces of pictures. Let your son take a look and make any changes to your design he thinks are necessary.

Once you've finalized the layout, lift each photo and tape it down. If you're using a frame, slide it in and voila! You've created a beautiful keepsake that's all the more special because you've made it together.

Make it harder: Add funny captions or speech balloons to each photo. Most photography stores sell blank stickers in the shape of speech balloons.

Make it easier: If your son is too young to use scissors, you can cut out the pictures for him, or buy a pocket photo album and let your son fill it with photographs.

TAKE IT APART

Most boys get a big kick out of taking things apart, especially electronics. The next time you buy a new phone, clock or radio, help your son explore the innards of the old one. Unplug the device, take the cover off with a screw driver and then let your son poke around inside and he'll no doubt find plenty of fascinating parts with which to tinker.

From miniature screws to LED displays and switches, the parts of most modern appliances are tiny, colorful and numerous—in other words, the perfect distraction for your son. If you know anything about electronics, explain what each part does and how the whole unit works together to perform its function, be it telling time, playing music or allowing you to talk to a friend on the other side of town. If the appliance you're disabling has an electric motor in it, show your son how it works by holding the connecting wires to the ends of a battery. Magnets, springs and gears are also fun to experiment with.

Once your son's curiosity is satisfied, keep the working parts for future projects. If he shows a special interest in any particular part of the appliance,

Materials Needed

- Old electronic devices
- Screwdriver
- Pliers

check out a book from the library learn more about it. Warning: some electronic components may contain toxins so don't smash open small parts and wash up carefully afterwards.

Make it harder: Once you take it apart, try to put it back together.

Make it easier: Little kids enjoy taking apart toys. Find a worn out toy in the basement and pull it apart with pliers.

TIME CAPSULE

E veryone wants to be remembered in the future. Help your kid leave a lasting legacy by creating a coffee can time capsule.

The first thing to do is gather bits of information, trinkets and other doodads that your son would like to put in the capsule. Explain to him that if you cut out and include newspaper or magazine articles, whoever discovers the package will be able to understand what your son's life was like. Suggest he include a family photo or two and make sure he identifies the people in the picture, the location and date on the back. He also might want to add something from his school—a newsletter or an assignment in which he did particularly well.

A recipe for his favorite dessert or an empty cereal box make good additions. Toss a few coins and stamps of recent vintage into plastic baggies (to protect them from wear) and put them in the time capsule. Tell your son that many people collect stamps or coins because they appreciate in value, so by the time someone uncovers the capsule, the coins or stamps might be more valuable.

Materials Needed

- Empty coffee can or other lidded container
- Note paper
- Trinkets
- Schoolwork
- Newspapers
- Coins
- Stamps
- Plastic baggies

Finally, have your son write a short note about himself, his family, hobbies and his school life. Mention that he should include his predictions for the future in the letter. If he's too young to write, pen it for him, but let him come up with its ideas.

Seal up the can with tape and then pick a burial spot. Under a tree, in your attic or in a crawl space in your house are great hiding places. Make a note of where it's buried in case you or your son want to search for it yourselves in 20 years.

Make it harder: Video tapes or audio tapes are fun additions to time capsules, if you want to spend a bit more time and energy.

Make it easier: Instead of the letter, have your son draw a picture of himself.

BREAKFAST IN BED

T here's nothing better than waking up to breakfast in bed. It's a simple treat that kids and adults alike enjoy. Best of all, it's an inexpensive, touching way to have your son show someone that he cares. Whether it's for Mom on Mother's Day or Grandpa on his birthday, your son will feel proud that he helped craft a delicious meal.

There's no rule that says the actual breakfast has to be fancy. A classic meal is often best, and pancakes are an easy fix. Buy your favorite pancake mix and follow the directions on the box. Let your son mix the ingredients together and add the mixture to the frying pan. Unless he's old enough, it's probably better if you actually make the pancakes.

While they are cooking, let your son prepare the tray. This is the most important part about serving breakfast

Materials Needed

- Pancake mix
- Milk
- Juice
- Fruit
- Serving tray
- Cutlery
- Dishes
- Flower

in bed, as it's all in the presentation. Use nice silverware and a special plate. Add a garnish to the main dish, such as a slice of melon or a peeled orange. Suggest that your son fold a cloth napkin for the tray and pour syrup and jam into small serving pitchers just like they do in restaurants. Add salt and pepper shakers if your meal calls for them and don't forget cream and sugar if you're serving coffee. If you have a garden, cut a few flowers as a final touch.

You'll probably have to carry the tray, but encourage your son to do an official wake-up call and announce your entrance. Breakfast isn't the same if you eat it alone, so be sure to make enough for you and your son too. That way you can all enjoy breakfast in bed! And don't forget to include your son in the clean up.

Make it harder: Use a recipe book and create a gourmet breakfast. Omelets and Eggs Benedict are two good ones to try.

Make it easier: Toasted bagels with cream cheese or peanut butter are meals just about anyone can make.

BUG COLLECTION

Boys love bugs. From creepy, crawly creatures to butterflies, grasshoppers and ladybugs, they're drawn to capturing, collecting and examining these natural specimens. Think like a kid for a few hours and join your son in his hunt for the perfect bug.

One of the first things you need to do when you are going on a bug hunt is to create a home for the creatures you catch. Any glass jar with a lid will do. Poke a few holes in the lid with a pair of scissors or a knife so air can circulate through the jar. Then head outside and let the adventure begin.

Start by adding some dirt, leaves and twigs into your jar. Then see what you can capture. Plenty of bugs hide under rocks or in the shallow soil beneath rotting logs. You'll probably see worms, pill bugs, ants and spiders. If you are lucky, you might catch sight of a cricket or grasshopper too.

Materials Needed
- A glass jar with lid
- Knife or scissors

Catching these little bugs is not always easy. Caterpillars, beetles, pill bugs, ladybugs and worms are probably your best bet. Some creatures can bite or sting, so make sure they're harmless before you reach out and pick them up. It's unlikely you'll be able to catch a butterfly without a net but it's much nicer to watch them flutter about the garden than to rest on a twig in your jar.

When you've caught your fill, spend an hour or two examining the bugs and their habits in their new home. Explain to your son how each of the insects has a special role in nature, be it to aerate the dirt, pollinate flowers or eat other, more harmful insects. Before you head back inside, encourage your son to release the creatures by unscrewing the lid and then putting the jar gently on its side in the grass. By doing this, you'll show him how to respect and love nature.

BIRD FEEDER

Introducing your child to nature at a young age lays the foundation for a lasting appreciation for his environment. And whether you live in a city or out in the countryside, birds of varying types call your neighborhood home. An easy way to get close to these feathery friends is by building a bird feeder.

Although there are many types of feeders, the easiest to manage, especially for younger boys, is the paper roll bird feeder. Start by poking two holes, one on either side of the tube, about half an inch down from the top. Thread a piece of yarn through the holes and tie a knot, creating a loop that serves as a hanger for the feeder.

Next, have your son smear peanut butter all over the tube, using a knife or his fingers. Spread a piece of wax paper on the table and pour birdseed evenly over the paper. Let your son roll the tube back and forth over the birdseed until it is completely covered. Poke a stick through the tube near the bottom to make a perch for feeding birds. And, voila! You have a completely biodegradable, tasty treat for local birds.

Materials Needed

- Empty paper towel or toilet paper roll
- Yarn
- Wax paper
- Peanut butter
- Birdseed

Try to hang the feeder near a window so you can watch the birds peck at the seeds. Find a bird guide at the library and help your son identify the sparrows, finches and other types of birds that use your feeder.

Remember, if you live in a cold climate, birds come to depend on you for a source of food, so make sure to replace your feeder regularly.

Make it harder: Make three bird feeders, using a different type of seed on each. Hang them in a row near each other and observe what types of birds prefer which type of seed.

Make it easier: Birds love seeds on anything, so if making the paper roll bird feeder is too much work for your son, have him just pour the seeds in a bowl and place it somewhere birds can easily get to it.

FAMILY STORY COLLECTION

Your family history can be just as important as what your son learns from a textbook at school. Help him recognize and appreciate relationships with his relatives by making a special collection of family stories.

Plan this activity around your child's desire to be creative. It can be an on-going project which you work on together whenever he feels like drawing or writing. It also makes a great gift for grandparents, cousins or even people within your immediate family.

Start the project by clearing a spot at the table and laying out pens, crayons and some paper for your son to use. Encourage your son to draw a picture depicting one of his favorite memories, be it a vacation you took, a baseball game with his cousins or his birthday last year. If he's old enough to write, he can include a description of the event somewhere on the drawing or on the back. Too young to sign his name? Help him by adding the text to his creation as he

Materials Needed

- Paper
- Pen
- Crayons
- Markers
- Hole punch
- Yarn

tells you what to write down. When you've finished for the day, store the picture or story in a box.

Add to the collection each time your son feels like it or you are looking for an activity to do together. If you'd like, you can contribute to the family history too by describing one of your favorite memories to your son and adding it to his project. Try to find the photos that go along with your memories and show your son so he can picture them.

Eventually your son will have a collection of simple, historic, stories about his family. Preserve the collection by laminating them and binding the pages with yarn. Make photocopies for distant relatives and friends. The collection will teach your son a bit about his own roots, and be something he can proudly show off at family gatherings.

Make it harder: Add photos or other mementos to the pages for a real "scrapbook" look.

MUSICAL INSTRUMENTS

Kids love making noise, whether it's banging pots together or rattling the keys of the family's baby grand. Tap into your son's inner musician by helping him make his own instruments.

One of the most melodious homemade music makers is a glass filled with water. Set up several glasses (wine glasses work best) and fill them with varying amounts of water. Have your son dip his finger in the water then gently rub it around the rim of the glass. As the water starts to vibrate, a pleasant tone will emanate from the glass. Each glass will provide a different pitch.

Materials Needed
- Empty coffee cans
- Dry beans
- Empty pop bottles
- Water glasses

Bottles can be the second instrument in your son's band. Start with an empty bottle—just about any bottle works—and have your son put his lips to the rim and blow straight across the opening. His effort will produce a gentle hum. Then add water to the bottle and see how the sound changes. Set up three bottles with different levels of water and suggest that he play a tune by moving from one to the other.

Perhaps the easiest instruments to make at home

belong to the percussion family. Coffee cans with plastic lids make fine drums. Add dry beans, tape the lid on, and you've got a maraca.

Once your son has "practiced" on all three instruments, join him for a concert. Put all the instruments on your kitchen table, decide who's going to play which, and choose a familiar tune to play. Before you know it the record companies will be knocking on your door.

Make it harder: A scale is composed of eight notes. Using a piano or other instrument as a guide to the pitches, have your son attempt to make a scale from eight bottles with varying levels of water.

Make it easier: Many kitchen items, from pots to cooking spoons, make great beginner "instruments" for little musicians.

FANCY SUMMER SHAKES

For a cool summer treat that doesn't require a trip to the ice cream store, prepare fruit shakes to drink after a tough day of playing in the hot sun. It's an easy task, and one in which your son can definitely participate.

Start by choosing what type of fruit you'd like to include in the shake. Suggestions include bananas, peaches, strawberries, blueberries, cantaloupe or other melon. You'll also need some milk, yogurt or if you'd prefer, vanilla ice cream. If you use ripe fruit (although you can use frozen as well), the shake should be sweet enough without adding sugar. But if you want to make it extra special, add cookie pieces or chocolate chips to the mix.

Materials Needed

- Blender
- Fruit
- Ice
- Milk
- Yogurt
- Glasses
- Straws

Lay the ingredients out on the table and let your son choose which ones he'd like. Explain that fruit is an important part of everyone's diet and encourage him to add plenty of it to the concoction. Next, ask your son to get about two cups of ice cubes from the freezer and pour them into the blender. Cut the selected fruit—one banana, one peach, half a cantaloupe or a cup of berries (or some similar combination)—into chunks and toss them in. Add one cup of milk, or half a cup of milk and half a cup of yogurt or ice cream.

Put the lid on and let your son do the blending, starting at a low speed and ending at a high speed. Blend until the mixture is smooth. If you are adding cookies or chocolate chips, add them now and blend at a low speed for a few seconds to stir them in.

Pour the shakes into tall glasses and add a straw to make drinking them more fun. Toast to summer days!

LEARNING BANK

Teaching your son the value of a dollar is something you should consider doing as soon as he realizes that money is more than just coins lying around in the spare change dish. Once he starts counting it, storing it in secret places and asking for ways in which he can obtain more of it, consider taking time out to teach your son how to "manage" his money.

This doesn't have to be a big, detailed project involving explanations about how to save now in order to afford college. Your son will probably have a difficult time imagining the distant future so it's best to keep things simple. Build your own Learning Bank at home that he can keep on a shelf or under his bed.

Take a shoe box and create three compartments by inserting two cardboard dividers into it, making each section 1/3 of the box. Put the lid back on the shoe box and cut three slots—big enough for him to be able to slip coins and bills through—one for each compartment. Then place a blank label just above each slot and designate the slots; Now (short term), Next Year (long term) and Charity. If you want to be more creative, let your

Materials Needed

- Shoe box
- Cardboard
- Scissors
- Pen
- Blank labels

son decorate the box with monetary symbols and coins from different countries.

Once your Learning Bank is complete, explain to your son what each compartment is for. The long term compartment, similar to a savings account, should be added to regularly but not used until he's saved up enough to buy something special, such as a new bike or a gift for someone. The short term compartment stores cash he can spend immediately, for trading cards, candy or small toys. The Charity compartment should hold the money he'd like to contribute to worthy causes such as a non-profit organization your family supports.

Your second task is to decide together how much

money he should put into each compartment. Your son should learn that to save money successfully, it has to become habit. The most important part in this activity is that when he banks his money, he contributes to each of the compartments. It's also smart to make sure that your tyke has goals for the money he is storing in his long term compartment. Otherwise he may not be eager to add money to that section. Encourage your son to use his Learning Bank by adding "interest" to his long term compartment.

Make it harder: Consider adding a fourth compartment called Family Contribution, which your son uses to help pay for a special family treat, such as a dinner out or an activity night out for the whole brood. Similar to the Charity compartment, this will teach him that sharing his earnings brings pleasure to others as well as himself.

Make it easier: If your son is too young to understand the concepts of money, start a Learning Bank for him, or let him collect change in a jar and use it to buy things that he wants.

TAKE A STAND

Being able to express opinions in a positive, straightforward manner is a good skill for anyone to have. Although your son's everyday life is probably limited to your neighborhood and his school, events that occur in other places in your city, region or country can affect him as well. And even though he may be too young to read the paper, he will still have opinions about newsworthy stories. Encourage these thoughts by teaching your son how to express his ideas on paper.

Explain to him that writing to a person in power, be it a local politician or the leader of the country, is an excellent way for citizens to get their voices heard. Start small. For example, if your son likes a particular restaurant, tell him that the proprietor of that restaurant would probably appreciate your son's comments. Help him compose a letter or do it for him if he's not old enough to write. Then, let him address the envelope, put on a stamp and drop it in the mailbox. Chances are your son will receive a response in short order, thanking him for his compliments. If he's lucky, the letter might

Materials Needed

• Writing paper and pen or word processor

even be framed and hung in the restaurant for all patrons to see.

Once he sees the affect a letter can have, encourage him to tackle larger issues. Does your son enjoy scrambling around at your local playground? Suggest he write the municipality and tell them how much he enjoys playing there. If the place needs more swings or a bigger sandbox, your son should include that in his letter too. Make sure he knows that he won't always get a response, but that doesn't mean he shouldn't make the effort. And if he's really ambitious, writing to the local paper is always a good way of expressing an opinion. He should include his name and age when he submits a letter and then keep your eyes peeled for its appearance in print.

This activity will help your son learn that the pen is mightier than the sword.

18

THE FAMILY TRIBUNE

Your son may not sit and read the paper with you on Saturday mornings, but there's no doubt he's watched you do it and has an idea of what it contains. Help him build an appreciation for reading up on current events by producing your own family paper.

The best part about this activity is that your son gets to act the part of editor, reporter, designer and printer while creating this paper. First, sit down and flip through a professional newspaper or two to see the layout and note how headlines are designed to catch your eye. Next, figure out a title for your paper, be it the *Family Tribune* or the *Blue House Gazette*. Once you're ready to go, put on the editor's hat.

As editor, your son should decide what stories go into the paper. Editors often come up with ideas for stories and then they send reporters out to glean information from the source. Is there anything new in the house—a pet, an appliance or a new toy? Has any family member done something interesting such as earn an A, make a friend or clean up the attic? Are there any important events coming up including birthdays, family vacations or a new baby?

Once you have a substantial list, let your son pick the four or five items that seem most interesting to him. In the notepad, write each story idea at the top of a separate piece of paper. Then, send your little reporter off to track down information on each of the topics he chose. Mention the five Ws (Who, What, Where, When, Why) so your son has a starting point for his investigation.

Suggest he take notes to more easily recall the facts he has learned.

Use the information he has uncovered to create good news stories. Begin with the most important and basic fact and fill in the details below, in order of importance. Once that's done, lay out the stories, with the most exciting article on the front page. Either type up the stories on the computer or have him copy the text neatly onto a sheet of blank paper. Make sure the text is written into columns (about half the width of a regular page). Then, cut out each story and have him arrange them artfully on a new piece of paper. Five stories should fill about two pages. Don't forget to leave room for the catchy headlines. If you'd like, cut out letters from an old newspaper and use them to spell out your headlines. Glue everything in place and presto! A family paper is born!

Print out copies on the computer or photocopy it so that friends and family can also enjoy your son's handiwork.

Make it easier: If your son can't write yet, ask him to dictate the news to you. After all, in the past reporters often dictated their stories to editors who did the actual writing.

OOBLECK

Slimy, sticky ooze. What kid wouldn't love playing with something that can be described using those words? This outrageous substance is a cinch to make and provides hours of fun for you and your tot.

To avoid creating a huge mess, spread newspaper on the floor around your kitchen table. Then, make sure your table is clear of anything that you don't want getting covered in goop. Set out two bowls and fill one with about a cup of water. Add a few drops of food coloring into the water and let your son stir it. Then, in a separate, large mixing bowl, add about eight ounces of corn starch. Give your son a mixing spoon and let him start stirring the corn starch. Slowly add some of the water, making sure he mixes as you pour. You want the consistency of the substance to be runny enough that it flows towards the lip as you tip the bowl, but feels solid when you tap it with a spoon. (Note: you might not need to add the whole cup of water.)

The beauty of this activity is that Oobleck exhibits properties of both a liquid and a solid. Pour it onto the table and you'll note that it looks similar to

Materials Needed

- Corn starch
- Water
- Food coloring
- 2 mixing bowls
- Spatula
- Newspaper

molasses as it spills out of the bowl. If you dip your spoon or fingers into it, however, the Oobleck immediately hardens. As you can imagine, playing with it turns into hours of amusement for your son.

Have your son hold out his hands over the table, fingers spread. Quickly flip the whole bowl of Oobleck over about six inches above his hands. The slimy substance will pour out in long, sticky strings through his fingers and onto the table. Once it makes contact with the table, it will begin running in slow streams towards the edges. Stop the streams with a spatula and watch it become hard and chalky. After a few moments, however, it will return to liquid form and spill past your spatula.

Try making balls, pancakes and other shapes with it or come up with your own experiments. When the fun is over, store the left over Oobleck in an air-tight container in the fridge.

Warning: Do not pour it down your drain. Also, although it is non-toxic, your son should not eat it.

PAPER AIR FORCE

Making paper airplanes is a quintessential activity for boys and it's a great way to have a lot of fun and learn a bit about aerodynamics at the same time. Paper airplanes have some important characteristics in common with their jet-powered brethren, as your son will learn when he starts launching his fleet. Among the similarities are the importance of broad wings to stay aloft and a sleek design to cut through the air.

Start with the most basic design. Take an 8.5" x 11" sheet of paper and fold it in half lengthwise. Lay it on the table in front of you with the long, open end at the top. Grasp the top right corner of the top flap and fold it all the way down so that what had been the right edge now lines up exactly with the bottom. Fold the top

right corner down on the bottom sheet, so it lines up exactly with the other corner you just folded. This creates the pointed "nose" of the plane.

With the paper still lying in front of you, fold the top of the paper down towards you, until about 1 inch of it hangs below the bottom of the paper, making one of the wings. Crease this fold, then flip the paper over and make the same fold on the other side.

Now fold up the wing tips about one quarter of an inch on each wing, and you're ready to fly! Hold the plane near the nose and gently send it gliding.

You can alter the flight by adding weight to the nose with paper clips, or by changing how the wings are folded. Experiment with different set-ups to see which works best. Complete your fleet by decorating the planes with markers, crayons and stickers.

Make it harder: Add a competitive aspect to your paper airplane adventure by having a contest to see whose plane can stay aloft the longest or travel the farthest.

Make it easier: Younger boys may not be able to successfully fold or fly the plane. Let them in on the fun by designating them chief decorators.

To Market

Parents usually find it easier to shop for groceries if the kids stay home. But it's not often that they have that luxury. To make shopping a fun expedition for you and your son, you've got to involve him in the process. You'll be amazed at how well behaved he is when he has a job to do.

Before you hit the local supermarket, ask him to help you make a list of items you will need. If he's old enough to write, let him pen the list. Then, sort through the tasks and figure out which ones he'll be able to carry out without too much difficulty. When you reach the store, hand him the list and let him keep the money in his pocket. Then, start at the top of the list and work your way down. As long as the items are not too high on the shelves, let your son add them to the shopping cart. Help him compare prices and choose the brands you family likes most.

Materials Needed

- Money
- Pen
- Paper

If you need something from the butcher, suggest that your son do the talking. Show him how to check the eggs to make sure there aren't any broken ones, and how to check labels to make sure the food you are buying is fresh. When you reach the checkout line, help your son unload the groceries and add up the money that you owe. Be sure to thank him for all his help.

Don't be shocked if the next time you mention shopping, your son eagerly offers his assistance.

TABLE HOCKEY

Diners, fast-food and neighborhood shops serve up the perfect opportunity for a game of table hockey while you wait for your meal. Success is guaranteed for those with a little hand-eye coordination and a competitive spirit. Just be sure to clear a space at the table away from glasses, cutlery and other diners.

Although the game will work with any three coins, quarters work best. Warm up with shooting practice. Arrange three quarters in an upside-down pyramid, so the tip points towards the player. Then, stab the tip of your index finger into the quarter closest to you. The other two quarters should shoot across the table. The harder you hit the first quarter, the farther the other quarters will slide.

Let your son practice this maneuver

Materials Needed

• 3 quarters

until he can do it with ease. Next, have your son create a "goal" at his side of the table by laying his hands flat on the table, thumbs extended to the sides. He should touch the tips of his thumbs together, creating a box with the top open (or a U shape). Have him put his thumbs along the edge of the table, positioning the "goal" directly opposite from you.

The next phase of the game is to move the "puck" across the "ice." Start by setting up an upside-down pyramid and knocking the quarter closest to you to send the other two quarters sliding. Then, advance the "puck" (the quarter closest to you) by shooting it through the other two quarters with your index finger. It must pass cleanly between them without touching either. The quarter nearest to you now becomes the "puck." Shoot that one through the gap between the other two and so on until you've crossed the table. Once you get close enough to the goal, pass the puck between the other two quarters and into the goal. Score!

The play switches to the other player if the shooter fails to put the rear quarter cleanly between the other two, or if any of the quarters fall off the table.

Make it harder: Tighten up the size of the goal by laying your thumbs side by side rather than tip to tip.

WATER FIGHT!

No local pool to dip your toes into on a swelter-
ing summer day? Try a water fight instead. Slip
on your swimming trunks, lather yourselves in
sunscreen and head outdoors for hours of refreshing
hijinks.

No matter how small your yard is, splashing about in
a sprinkler is always a joy for kids. Classic
squirt guns still hold appeal for the
younger set, and they are as inexpensive
as you can get. Don't have time for a trip
to the store to pick up supplies? Use
rinsed out detergent or spray bottles to
soak each other. Make the game more of
a challenge by limiting your target to a
specific body part, such as the foot or an
elbow.

Materials Needed

- Squirt guns
- Spray bottles
- Hose
- Sprinkler
- Balloons

Water balloons are fun to play with too. Try tossing
one back and forth, taking a step back each time you
make a throw. Eventually someone will drop it and get
drenched! When you've had enough, towel off and
enjoy relaxing in the shade with a tall glass of lemonade.

Make it harder: Have a contest to see who can shoot a

stream of water from a squirt bottle or squirt gun the farthest.

(24)

GEAR POUCH

Boys grow so quickly, clothes are often too small long before they are worn out. The next time your son outgrows a pair of pants, recycle them by making a gear pouch.

Any pair will do, but jeans work best. Lay them on the table and draw a line across one of the legs with a marker, about a foot above the cuff. Let your son cut along the marked line. When he's done, turn the tube of material inside out. Thread a needle with durable thread and tie the ends of the thread together. If he's old enough, demonstrate with a few stitches and then let your son do the rest. Sew up one end of the tube (leaving the cuff side open). Then, turn it right side out.

Materials Needed

- Old pair of pants
- Scissors
- Needle
- Thread
- Markers
- Craft supplies

Once the pouch part is finished, cut a thin strip about a foot long from the remaining part of the pant leg. In a few quick stitches, attach the end of the thin strip to the pouch about two inches from the open end. This will serve as your tie to hold the pouch closed.

Using markers, glue, felt, beads, buttons or fabric paint, have your son decorate the pouch to his own taste. Then it's ready to store his rock collection, toy cars or whatever else of value he wants to protect.

Make it harder: If your son is handy with a needle have him add buttons or a zipper to the top instead of the tie. It will be a little classier.

TREASURE HUNT

Whether it's just you and your son or a whole pile of youngsters at a birthday party, hunting for hidden treasure is always a treat. Discovering and decoding clues helps your tyke learn valuable problem solving skills in an enjoyable, exciting way.

Be sure to create the clues ahead of time and set up the game when he is not around. Clues should be kept relatively simple. If you make them too challenging, your son will get frustrated and lose interest in the game. Try hiding clues in everyday places such as the mailbox, under the couch or in the fridge. Each clue should direct you to the next hiding place. If you have the time, draw a map with an X that marks the spot where the loot is buried. Hide the map as the last clue and your little explorer will get a kick out of navigating his way to the treasure. It's also a good idea to have a hint or two ready in case he gets stuck. When he finds the treasure (candy or a small toy work well), suggest he share it with you or his siblings.

Playing with a group of kids? Divide them into teams

Materials Needed
- Paper
- Pen
- Treasure

and make sure there is treasure enough for everyone. For a change of pace, help your son prepare and hide the clues. He'll derive just as much pleasure watching someone else struggle to figure out the clues as hunting for the treasure himself.

(26)

SNOWFLAKES

Whether you live in the north or south, snow is something children love to think about. The white, fluffy flakes that tumble down from the sky make perfect snowballs, snow people and surfaces for sledding. If it's not the season for snow or there's no white stuff where you live, make your own by creating paper snowflakes.

Start by cutting a stack of paper into squares. Then, take a sheet and fold the top right corner to the bottom left corner, making a triangle. Fold the triangle in half. Then, let your son cut out shapes from each of the three sides. Try cutting out different shapes such as diamonds and rectangles. Let him use a hole punch to cut out circles from the middle. Once he's

Materials Needed
- Paper
- Scissors
- Decorating supplies
- Hole punch
- Thread or yarn

finished, unfold the paper and marvel at his snowflake. Explain to him that no two snowflakes that fall from the sky are exactly alike. Each is unique, just like the ones he is making. For added fun, fold the paper more than twice before cutting it.

Decorating snowflakes are just as enticing as making them. Try dipping the whole thing in glue and then dusting it with glitter. Or, paste sparkling stars to each snowflake. Combine some water-based paint with water and have your son soak his snowflake in the mixture. As the paint dries, it creates interesting patterns of color. You can even draw on the paper beforehand and then cut a snowflake out of the masterpiece.

Once you've finished, poke a hole in the top of each with the hole punch and thread string or yarn through them and hang them in your front window. Have a blizzard in June!

(27)

OLD MAN APPLES

For an art project that "does its own thing," make apple faces and watch them age right before your eyes!

Peel the skin from some apples. Next, take a knife, spoon or flat tool and carve facial features into each apple. If your son is very young, you might ask him to describe the features to you while you try your hand at carving. The deeper you carve, the more pronounced your apple face will be when it dries. Try adding tiny beads for eyes and dry pieces of spaghetti for teeth.

Once you've finished creating, soak the little apple heads in salt water for several hours. This prevents them from rotting. Remove them from the water, pat them dry and set the apple heads

Materials Needed

• Apples
• Salt
• Cotton
• Beads
• Spaghetti
• Craft supplies
• String
• Paper clips

on a windowsill or shelf where you and your son can see them.

Over the course of the next few weeks as your apples lose moisture, the faces will slowly transform to look like wrinkly, shriveled old men. Once they've stopped shrinking, add accessories such as glasses or a hat using paper clips, bottle caps, felt and other craft supplies. Give your old man head a moustache, a beard or hair with bits of string or cotton. Wrap them up for gifts or keep the little guys around somewhere visible. Their wizened appearance is always good for a smile.

Make it harder: Create puppets by sticking a wooden skewer into the apple head before you soak it in salt water. While the head is "aging," make clothes, hands and feet for your puppet out of material, felt, buttons, ribbon and other odds and ends. When the apple has shrunk, sew or glue the clothes onto the skewer near the base of the head. Make sure you can hold onto the skewer to move your puppet around.

28

HORROR BOWLS

There's more to Halloween that free candy. Help your son get into the spirit of the season by setting up a haunted house. Whether it's in your basement or right by the front door, the trick to spooking up your home is creating Horror Bowls. They're a simple and fun way to make it a howling Halloween.

Start by boiling some water and adding spaghetti. While it's cooking, you and your son can peel the skin from about 20 grapes. It's easiest if you use a knife, but it's possible to do it with your fingers. Fill the rubber glove with water and tie a knot at the "wrist" so the liquid can't escape. When the spaghetti is done, drain and rinse it in cold water.

Let your son place each of the items in one of the large bowls. Cover each bowl with aluminum foil and have your son punch a fist-sized hole through the top of each. Set the bowls out in a darkened area and then send your tyke off to lure his first "victim" to the bowls of horror. Each victim should try to guess what the bowls contain by sticking their hand through the hole and feeling around. Encourage your son to give

Materials Needed

- 3 large bowls
- Aluminum foil
- Grapes
- Cooked spaghetti
- Rubber glove

detailed accounts of each bowl's contents: eyeballs, brains and a severed hand.

If you want to go all out, add creepy music, spider webs, hanging ghosts (made from white sheets) and leering jack-o-lanterns to the mix. You and your son will get a kick out of frightening even your bravest guests.

29

FAMILY CALENDAR

Keeping the family organized, especially if everyone is involved in a variety of activities, is no easy task. But there's a way your son can help get everything under control. Track everyone's schedule with a homemade calendar.

Start by folding each sheet of paper in half. Then, place the paper in a stack (one inside the other) so the folds line up. Next, staple along the fold through the seven sheets so that they are all attached (two or three staples should do). You now have a blank calendar.

Press along the fold so that the pages will turn more easily. Then, with the folded, stapled part facing away from you, flip it open. The bottom half of the page is reserved for the calendar for the month of January. The upper segment is for the picture representing that month. Using a ruler and a black marker, create a grid for the days of the week and fill in the dates according to the upcoming year. Leave enough room at the top of the page to write January. Repeat this on each page for each month of the year. You'll

Materials Needed

- 7 sheets of white paper (11" x 17"
- Family photographs
- Markers
- Tape
- Stapler
- Ruler

have three blank pages at the end to use for phone numbers, addresses or notes.

Once the tough part is done, the fun begins! Let your son decorate the cover and each month with family photographs, drawings, collage, stickers, sparkles and any other art supplies he might enjoy using. Encourage him to create pictures that correspond to the month in question. If he's decorating October, for example, pumpkins and ghosts might be in order.

Finished decorating? Now it's time to add important dates into the calendar, such as family members' birthdays, holidays, the first day of school, vacations and anything else that might be special to your son. You can spice these up too, by adding photos, stickers or fancy writing.

Hang the calendar in a prominent place in your house or suggest your son wrap it up and give it to a close family member as a present. Either way, he'll be able to ogle his masterpiece day after day, and you might just find yourselves a little less likely to forget important events.

Make it harder: Have your son plan a completely different design for each month. For example, a photo collage for January; finger paints for February; colored paper collage for March.

Make it easier: Choose a photo for each month and

tape that on yourself. Then have your son decorate the border.

(30)

MATH OLYMPICS

I s your son is a budding mathematician? Or is he little overwhelmed by arithmetic? Either way, he'll enjoy playing Math Olympics. Shhh! Just don't tell him it's educational.

This simple activity can be adjusted to match your son's abilities. Similar to the Olympic pentathlon, this game has five events; addition, subtraction, division, multiplication and patterns. Prepare ahead of time by writing 100 problems (20 per category) on note cards with the questions on one side, the answers on the other. Each category should contain problems with varying degrees of difficulty. Assign a point value to each card from 1 to 20, with the easiest question receiving one point and the most difficult question receiving 20.

When compiling questions for the "patterns" category, the goal is to help your son recognize relationships between numbers. For example, your

Materials Needed

• Note cards
• Pen

one-point question could ask him to predict the next number in the series (1, 2, 3, 4...). Five is the right answer. To make them harder, try this example: 2, 4, 8, 16... (the answer is 32, as each consecutive number is double that which precedes it).

Once the game is ready, explain the rules to your son and away you go. Younger children especially enjoy starting with the easiest questions. You can go through an entire set of questions before moving on to the next category or mix it up by asking him sets of five questions (one from each category). Keep track of the points he earns for answering correctly. There are a total of 1,050 possible points. Three hundred points earns him a bronze medal, 500 a silver and anything over 800 is gold. For fun, make up three medals out of cardboard, crayons and string and award him the appropriate honor when you've completed the game.

Make it harder: Ask him to turn the tables and create his own set of cards to test your skills. It will be a challenge for him to make sure each answer is correct.

Make it easier: If basic math is still too much for your son, try a pentathlon that tests his knowledge of counting, colors, shapes, days of the week and basic vocabulary.

31

KEEP IN TOUCH

In this day and age, there are many ways to keep in touch with friends and family who you don't see often, from e-mail to phone calls to letters. If there's someone special who your son would like to correspond with, however, consider recording a tape as a means of communication. It's a simple, unique and personal way to show how much you care.

To have a finished product that your son is proud of, do a little pre-planning. Discuss what he'd like to share with the tape's recipient. Help him jot down a few notes about what he's going to talk about. Then encourage him to get creative by including plenty of sounds to make it more interesting. Singing, playing an instrument, recording his sibling's voice, reading a poem and catching the family pet on tape are all excellent additions.

Materials Needed

- Tape recorder
- Blank tape
- Markers
- Photos
- Envelope
- Stamps

Write out a rough "script" which includes topics of conversation and the approximate placement of the various sound effects. Then, press record and let your son go at it. It's a good idea if he greets the recipient first and explains what he is doing and why. Let him ramble, tell jokes, talk about school, family, friends, sports and whatever other parts of his life he wants to share. Include the sounds and you've got a fantastic gift!

It's a good idea to listen to the tape before you mail it. Encourage your son to comment on the success of the project and together come up with ways you can make it better. Decorate the cassette liner with drawings and photos and include a title. Then, make a copy of the tape for you to keep in case the original gets lost. Wrap the package securely and send it along.

Make it harder: Have your son take the tape recorder around your house and "interview" his siblings or parents. Or, have him take it to school, the playground or friends' houses. Each of these additions will make the tape a more complete record of your son's life.

Make it easier: Record your son's imaginative ramblings. The recipient will still love it.

32

FALL COLORS

In northern climates, fall is a time to admire the beautiful colors that cooler weather brings. Capture the deep reds, oranges, golds and browns of the season with a simple leaf craft. If you hang it in your house, your son will be able to relive the experience of fall all year round.

Take a stroll through your neighborhood and pick up a few very colorful leaves. It's best if these leaves are not brittle. Bring your leaf collection home and set it out on the table. Then, have your son choose four or five crayons in his favorite colors. Peel the paper from the bottom of each crayon and grate the colored wax into slivers, using a knife or grater. You'll soon have a pile of colorful shavings.

Tear off a sheet of wax paper that is about twice the width of the leaf. Lay it on a towel on a table (or on an ironing board) with the waxy side up. Now have your son artfully arrange the leaf and the shavings on the wax paper. Tell him to sprinkle some shavings on the leaf, but most should fall on the wax paper.

Put another sheet of wax paper on top

Materials Needed

- Crayons
- Leaves
- Wax paper
- Iron
- Knife or grater
- Hole punch
- String or yarn
- Scissors

of the whole creation, wax side down. With your iron set at a low temperature, gently press down on the top sheet. In a few moments the paper will become crystal clear, the crayon shavings will melt into an amazing design, and the whole thing will become stuck together.

Set it aside to cool for a few minutes. Then cut out the best part of the design with scissors, perhaps in a leaf shape. For an added touch, punch a hole through the top and tie a loop of string in it. Now your son can hang his permanently colorful fall leaf in his room.

Make it harder: Rather than choosing one leaf, have your son find one from each tree in your yard. Mount them all and include little slips of paper identifying each leaf.

Make it easier: If leaves are in short supply, consider a construction paper leaf instead.

33

SURF THE WEB

Computers, the Internet and the World Wide Web have become the wave of the future. Spending an hour or two in front of a computer with your son will help him get a leg up on the information superhighway. And, it may surprise you. He might just teach you a thing or two.

Even if you don't have a computer at home, many schools, libraries and Internet cafés offer Internet access for free or a nominal fee. Start by giving your son a quick lesson about what the Web is. Explain that the phone line or cable connects the computer you are using with millions of other computers. Because all these computers are sharing information, you and your son can access many resources and interesting sites at the click of a button.

Materials Needed

• A computer with an Internet connection

Click onto a search engine and ask your son to type in something he'd like to learn about. Using a few key words is easier than writing a whole sentence. You'll both be amazed at the wealth of information the engine uncovers. You can also try playing on-line games, listening to music or watching trailers for the latest

movies you'd like to see together. If your son has been learning how to use the computer at school, let him show you sites he's visited and activities he's participated in. Or, open a free e-mail account and let him send messages to friends and family. Pretty soon your son will be surfing all by himself. Just be warned that while there are plenty of sites that are kid-specific, many are also geared to an older crowd.

Make it harder: If your son is old enough to write, he may enjoy participating in chat groups on topics he's interested in. Introduce your son to this feature of the Web, but be sure to monitor his conversations.

Make it easier: Just go to a fun kids' game site and let your son at it.

34

WHAT AM I?

Boys love to make-believe. Stimulate their imaginations by playing the game in which they get to pretend to be different people, places and things. Commonly called Charades among the older set, kids of any age get a kick out of this modified version.

In What am I?, each person playing the game takes a turn to silently act out a character or object through gestures. The other players try to guess what the actor is trying to be. Start by each taking five sheets of paper and writing down the names of movies, famous people, places, books and everyday objects. Once each player has come up with five, fold them into squares and put them in a hat (if there are only two of you playing, add ten or more).

Materials Needed

- Hat
- Pens
- Strips of paper

Take turns drawing a slip of paper from the hat and acting out what it says on the paper. Try to keep them simple enough that your son can do them on his own. The "actor" can start his charade by announcing whether the genre is movie, book, object or person. He should try his best to describe what it says on the paper without using words.

The audience is encouraged to yell out guesses until they hit upon the right answer. If, after several minutes they cannot guess it, the actor may throw out hints, such as color, size, whether the subject is animate and so forth. If everyone gives up, the actor should announce what his subject was. Encouragement and compliments on your son's acting abilities will make this game more fun and enjoyable for everyone.

Make it harder: Try limiting the potential characters to those found in books you've recently read. It will force your son to remember, and may make him listen better the next time you read together.

STUFFED ANIMAL PARTY

Kids love copying what their parents do and if you're the type to throw parties, it's likely your son will get a kick out of hosting his own "stuffed animal" shindig.

This activity can be as complicated or as simple as you want to make it. For the serious host, invitations

Materials Needed

- Stuffed animals
- Other assorted toys
- Snacks

and party decorations are in order. If it's your son's first time, having him announce the Stuffed Animal Party is probably enough. Help him collect the "guests" and bring them to the party. Teach him proper party manners by showing him how to introduce the guests to each other, taking coats and bringing around tidbits of food and drink. Let him be in charge of the action and offer to assist him as necessary.

Playing board or card games, dancing and getting dressed up are good things for your son to do with his friends at the party. Spice up the action by serving a special treat such as sparkling apple juice (club soda and apple juice) and sandwiches with the crusts cut off. And be sure to make sure your son knows that when all his guests leave, the host always cleans up the mess before bed!

BACKSTAGE

Been to the zoo, playground and toy store too often lately? For a change of pace, consider visiting a local establishment to learn what goes on "backstage."

Plenty of places around town will be more than happy to show you around. Most local newspapers, radio and television stations have formal tours available where your son can ogle the massive printing machines, visit a sound booth and see the amazing amount of audiovisual equipment it takes to produce a television program. If your daily paper doesn't host tours, try the weekly community paper. You'll probably be the first people to visit!

If your son is more interested in culinary delights, factory tours are always a hit. Plenty of factories have special tours for interested guests and the visit often includes tasty samples of the product they are manufacturing. No factories nearby? Try the local fire station. Dads and sons alike enjoy inspecting the hook and ladder trucks, emergency vehicles, uniforms, equipment and living quarters of firefighters. Most fire-houses are delighted to give a brief lesson or two on fire safety while you are visiting.

Dropping in on your town hall or city's government chambers can be both educational and eye opening. It's probably a good idea to find out when the governing body is going to be in session to see a bit of the action. You might want to explain what your local mayor does before you head in, just so your son knows what to expect.

There are a plethora of other options right in your own neighborhood. The key to enjoying this activity together is choosing an establishment that does something or provides a service that your son is interested in, such as television or police work. Make an appointment and spend an hour or two learning about the businesses in your community.

37

MAGIC SHOW

What kid isn't awed by slight-of-hand card tricks, rabbits popping out of hats and disappearing acts? Fuel your son's desire to become a magician by helping him create his own magic show. Younger siblings will be amazed by their big brother's ability to perform magic.

The staple of any show is the Find-the-Card trick. Take any deck of cards, shuffle it and quickly glance at the bottom card. Have someone from your audience draw a card and tell him or her to replace it on the bottom of the deck. Then, make a big show of shuffling the cards (but in actuality you should shuffle very lightly). Flip through the stack until you find the card that was originally at the bottom of the deck. The next card should be the one selected by your audience member. Pull it out with a flourish and announce your find!

Materials Needed

- Deck of cards
- Carrot
- Pin
- Handkerchief
- Lotion

The second trick to learn is the Pin-in-the-Finger ploy. Begin by hiding a carrot up your sleeve. Pull a long handkerchief out of your pocket and announce that you have discovered a magic formula for making fingers impervious to pain. Next, dip your finger into the magic potion (a small dish of skin lotion) and rub it in. Then, slip the handkerchief over your hand with your index finger pointing up. Quickly swing your arm down by your side to let the carrot fall from your sleeve into your hand. Under the handkerchief, replace your finger with the carrot. Bring your arm back up and dramatically stab your "finger" with a pin. As the audience "oohs" and "ahhhs," remove the pin and slip the carrot into your pocket. Reveal your unbloodied finger.

Finally, wrap up your show by announcing that some dust must have gotten into your eye. Explain to the audience that you need to clean your eyeball. With your index finger, pretend to scoop out one eyeball, quickly closing that eye. Pretend to pop your eyeball into your mouth, and, using your tongue, swish it around in your mouth. Pull it back out and "replace" it in its socket. Open that eye and deem it a successful cleaning.

The success of a magic show depends more on showmanship than the actual tricks, so have your son practice in front of you or a mirror before the show. Help him make a magic wand out of a pencil wrapped in black construction paper and a long cape out of spare material. Make fancy signs announcing your son's show and set up a table with a black cloth covering it for his "props." If he can't get enough, visit the library and spend time learning new magic tricks together.

38

BEACH MEMORIES

Is your son a beach bum? Did he spend hours playing in the sand on your last trip to the lake or ocean? If so, he'll love creating a diorama to keep those memories close to his heart.

Most boys enjoy collecting things, especially items they find on the beach such as shells, colorful stones, beach glass, driftwood and sand dollars. Encourage your son to sort through his treasures and pick a variety of his favorites. Next, mix the concrete according to the instructions. It's probably a good idea to wear clothing you don't mind getting dirty and doing this activity outdoors or in a workshop. When the concrete is ready, pour it into the pie plate, to a depth of about one inch.

Now it's your son's turn. Let him arrange his beach items in the pan. Try re-creating a beach scene or making a pattern with large and small shells. Once all the treasures are in position, sprinkle a thick layer of sand over the whole pan so it sticks to any cement that is still exposed. Wait for a few moments and then pour off the excess sand. Let the mixture dry overnight.

Materials Needed

- Quick-set concrete (without stones)
- Sea shells and other beach treasures
- Sand
- Aluminum pie plate

As the cement hardens, it should shrink slightly, making it easy to pop out of the aluminum when it is finished. Display the diorama on your patio or use it as a paperweight. Either way, your son will remember the good times he had at the beach every time he spots his masterpiece.

Make it harder: Create a hanger for the diorama by poking the hook end of a wire coat hanger through the bottom of the pan before adding the cement. Bend the rest of the coat hanger so it is spread roughly evenly through the pan. The hook will allow you to hang the diorama on the wall when it's done, and the rest of the hanger will be reinforced in the concrete.

Make it easier: Clay or plaster of Paris will also work, if you don't want the hassle of mixing cement.

(39)

BOARD GAME

B oys think board games are a blast, so imagine how much your son will enjoy playing a game he created!

First, you and your son are going to have to decide what the goal of your game will be. The simplest way to play is to declare the first one to reach a certain point the winner. Other options include amassing points or seeing one's pieces safely around the board.

The next step is to decide the method of moving pieces around the board. Many board games use dice so it's likely you have a pair kicking around just waiting to be used. Or, you

Materials Needed

- Paper
- Dice
- Crayons
- Cardboard or construction paper

could make a set of cards with advancement directions such as "move ahead two spaces" or "go back to the red square." Let your son decide which method he prefers.

Finally, pick a theme for your board game. Be it dinosaurs, buildings, sports or reading, your son should choose something he's interested in so playing the game will be personal and fun. Once you've decided on a theme, it's time to design and build the board.

Start with a large sheet of construction paper or cardboard. Draw a trail of squares (or triangles, circles or diamonds) that lead from Start to Finish (unless you are using another method such as amassing points). Once the path to victory is complete, fill in the squares with items relating to your theme—"Break your bat - lose a turn," or "Find a fossilized egg - roll again." Alternatively, the spaces can direct you to perform certain actions or draw from your set of cards. Add decorations pertaining to your theme and write down the rules on a piece of paper. Then, let the game begin!

CAR WASH

Car starting to look like it could use a wash? Instead of taking it to your local car wash (which is a great activity in its own right), plan an afternoon of scrubbing with your tyke. Gather up the hose, sponges, dish soap and some clean rags. Dress in bathing suits or clothes you don't mind getting wet and head outside for some sudsy fun.

Materials Needed

- Sponges
- Dish soap
- Bucket
- Rags

Your son will like plying the hose so suggest he start by hosing down the car and then filling the bucket with water as you add in dish soap. Hand your son a sponge and assign him a spot of the car to scrub clean. After he's finished that section of the car, inspect it carefully and

praise him for a job well done. Have him rinse off cleaned areas as they pass inspection. You'll probably have to do the roof, but most every other part of the car is within your son's reach. Let him do as much as he wants, and finish off what he can't.

Hose down the car one last time, then use rags to "polish" it to a nice shine. Once the car is done, hop in and drive your clean vehicle through town so your son can show off his hard work. Treating your little worker to an ice cream cone might be in order.

(41)

SNOW ART

When the grey days of winter start getting you down, transform the bland landscape into a sea of color with some water and food coloring.

Rinse out a few empty spray bottles (household cleaners work well) and then fill them halfway with water. Let your son add a few drops of food coloring to each, twist the cap on and shake them up. Bundle up, head outside and let your imagination

Materials Needed

• Empty spray bottles
• Food coloring
• Water

run wild.

Experimenting on a patch of snow is a good idea before you start your masterpiece. See what happens when you spray colored water from different distances. Try mixing colors by spraying one onto the snow and then covering it with a second. Hold one bottle in each hand and spray both colors together. Which method does your son like best?

Once you've got the technique down, there are a thousand things to color. Build a snowperson and "paint" on a scarf, hat, buttons and shoes. Spray paint your name into a snow bank. Consider the snow as your canvas and decorate your lawn with holiday drawings. If you'd like to make your paintings last longer, add

more color to your creation after it freezes over night. Try using hot water the second time and watch how the frozen colors thaw and mix with new colors.

42

COOKIE COOK

Baking cookies is a messy, tasty treat that boys love. Although pre-packaged dough is simpler, making cookies from scratch can be a more satisfying endeavor, especially for older children who enjoy measuring, sifting and stirring.

Don aprons first, and roll up any sleeves that might get in the way of the baking process. Let your son collect the ingredients and lay them out on the table or counter where you will be working. Beat butter and shortening with an electric mixer for 30 seconds (or with a wooden spoon for about four minutes) until the batter is smooth. Add sugar, one egg, milk, baking powder, vanilla and about half the flour. Mix well. Add the rest of the flour and stir until all ingredients are mixed.

This recipe works best if the batter is allowed to chill in the fridge for an hour or two. Use the break to clean up the mess you've made, wash the dishes and put the ingredients away. If you are going to put icing on your

Materials Needed

- Rolling pin
- Cookie cutters
- Baking sheet
- Mixing bowl
- Wooden spoon
- Measuring utensils
- Cooling rack
- Oven mitts
- Aprons
- Electric mixer (optional)

cookies, this is a good time to make it. (Icing: combine one cup of powdered sugar with 1/4 teaspoon of vanilla in a small bowl. Stir in one tablespoon of milk at a time until it is the right consistency). You can also pre-heat the oven to 375°F.

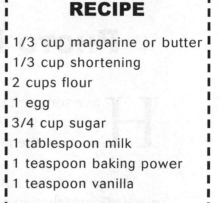

RECIPE

1/3 cup margarine or butter
1/3 cup shortening
2 cups flour
1 egg
3/4 cup sugar
1 tablespoon milk
1 teaspoon baking power
1 teaspoon vanilla

Sprinkle a little flour on a smooth surface. Take the cookie dough out of the fridge and separate it in half. Lay one half on the floured surface. Roll your rolling pin in flour and then use it to flatten the dough until it's about 1/8th of an inch thick. At this point, your son can cut out shapes in the dough using cookie cutters or a butter knife. Encourage creativity!

Set the cut cookies on the ungreased baking sheet and have your son sprinkle on sugar, chopped nuts or little candies for decoration. Bake for seven or eight minutes until the edges are firm and the bottom is lightly browned. Remove them from the sheet and cool them on a rack or cutting board. Frost and enjoy!

43

PHOTO DECORATIONS

Have some left over of wallet-sized school photos of your son? Instead of storing them in a drawer, turn them into decorations for the holiday season.

Using a pencil, have your son trace his hand on a piece of construction paper. Cut out the hand shape and glue his photo to the "palm." With glitter, stickers, crayons, markers and glue, add creative designs around the photo. Write his name and date on the back of the hand. Then, punch a hole in the construction paper and thread a length of string or ribbon through the hole. Hang this handy decoration from your mantle.

Want to make something a little more intricate? Cut eight strips of construction paper (eight inches long and one inch wide). Let your son arrange two strips end to end, overlapping the ends one inch. Next, lay two more strips perpendicular to the first two so their ends overlap at the same point where the first strips overlap (you should have a large cross shape with the overlapping ends in the middle). Arrange the final four strips at angles with their

Materials Needed

- Construction paper
- Stapler
- Wallet-sized photos
- String

ends stacking up in the center. When you are finished placing the strips, you should have a star pattern. Put a staple through the entire stack of overlapping ends. Now, fold each strip towards the center and staple it all together. Glue your son's photo in the middle of this sunburst (over the staples). Tie a piece of string through one of the loops and presto! Your son is the star of your holiday festivities.

(44)

LEMONADE STAND

D o you have fond memories of selling lemonade on the corner for five cents a glass? Indulge in a little nostalgia by helping your son set up his own lemonade stand. He'll learn the rudiments of running a business and pocket a few dollars as well.

Hot days work best for business. And while a busy street corner might be more economically viable, setting up right in front of your house is usually your best option. Start by finding a table and chair your son can use as his

Materials Needed

- Small table
- Chair
- Lemonade
- Pitcher
- Paper or plastic cups
- Change
- Marker
- Cardboard

stand. Set them up on the sidewalk and then have your son make a sign to promote his business: "Lemonade—25 cents" should do the trick. Stack the cups neatly and use a table cloth to make things look more professional.

Now it's time to make the product. Head inside and find the biggest pitcher you have. If you want to go all out, make your own using the recipe above. (Combine four cups cold water with sugar in a sauce pan over high heat. Boil for five minutes until syrupy mixture turns clear. Remove from heat and cool.

In pitcher, combine lemon juice, syrup and six cups of water. Stir and serve). You can also use dry mix or lemonade from concentrate. Add ice cubes to keep it cool and your son is ready for his first customer.

Make sure your son has enough quarters, dimes and nickels to give correct change.

RECIPE

2 cups granulated sugar
4 cups cold water
3 cups freshly squeezed lemon juice
6 cups cold water, seltzer or sparkling water

Explain that if he is polite and courteous to his customers, they will likely come back for seconds or bring their friends. Then, retire into the background and let your son do the work. A little entrepreneur is born!

Make it harder: Explain that in a real business, the key to success is selling the product for more than it costs to acquire or produce. Figure out roughly how much it costs to make one cup of lemonade, and ask your son how much he thinks he should charge for a cup. Don't forget to take materials such as cups and napkins into consideration.

(45)

OBSTACLE RACE

L ooking for a fun way to get your son away from the computer or television? Suggest that you build an obstacle course together. He'll be sure to jump at the chance to engage in a friendly competition with Dad and burn some energy along the way!

This activity is great for even your youngest tot. Start by picking a location (yard, basement, attic, playground or other appropriate place) and plan out the route together. Avoid potentially dangerous obstacles such as low-hanging branches or ceiling beams. Once you've established a path, it's time to come up with the obstacles you will need to overcome in order to reach the finish line. There are two kinds you can incorporate into your game; natural or fabricated structures you need to jump over, crawl under and swing on, and tasks you need to accomplish at a particular point in the race.

If you have a swing set, sandbox or jungle gym, fit them into your race. Use ride-on toy vehicles to get from point A to B. Set up a log to walk along or hop over. If there is snow on the ground, make a pile or tunnel to climb over or scoot through. Once the obstacles are established, throw in a few tasks. At one station, have your son spin around three times before he can continue. You can also add jumping jacks, throwing a ball at a target, hopping, skipping, somersaults or any other activity you can think of.

Now you are ready for action! Run the "gauntlet" separately or together. Which ever way you choose to compete, cheer wildly as your champ makes his way through the course.

Make it harder: Throw a few mental tasks into the course. Have him count backwards from 25 after tackling the log jump, say the alphabet while somersaulting, or name the last three winners of the World Series while he pitches a ball.

RECYCLED CITY

The great thing about participating in a recycling program is that the container you use to store your "trash" is often filled with treasures just waiting to be put to use. Empty coffee cans, cardboard boxes and tubes, milk cartons and jars are perfect materials to create a miniature play city.

Gather your supplies (make sure they are clean!) on the table or floor. It's a good idea to use a large piece of cardboard or poster board as the "ground" for your city. If your son wants to make this a big production, use a crayon to trace out roads and sidewalks and designate positions for your buildings just like an urban planner would. Consider including alleys, airports, bridges and industrial parks.

Materials Needed

- Whatever happens to be in your recycling box (cereal boxes, coffee cans, paper towel tubes)
- Scissors
- Crayons
- Glue

Next, use your recycled materials to create the buildings. Tubes make excellent skyscrapers and smokestacks. Cereal boxes are perfect for factories, apartment buildings and schools. Coffee cans make good airport control towers and office buildings. Use a jar as your city's water tower.

Cut out windows and doors and decorate your buildings with construction paper, crayons and other craft supplies. Glue your creations in their appropriate place and add trees, cars and people. Color the base green to simulate grass and the roads black.

Make it harder: Get a picture of the skyline of the nearest large city and have your son try to duplicate it with the recycled materials.

Make it easier: You can make the buildings and base, and have your son just place them. His play cars and action figures can make excellent inhabitants of the city.

(47)

ROCK COLLECTION

Boys have a penchant for collecting things, especially rocks. Encourage your son's hobby by helping him build a fancy box in which to showcase his collection.

Before you can build a display case, your son will need to go hunting for rocks. Depending where you live, you might find rocks in the driveway, backyard, beach, stream or local park. (Most nature preserves prohibit the removal of any natural objects.) It's likely that while you are searching, your son will gravitate to the biggest rocks. Try to draw his eye to smaller, more colorful stones as well. They are easier to carry and often are more interesting than the big ones. Encourage your son to seek variety rather than quantity.

Materials Needed

- Shoe box
- Rocks
- Craft glue
- Markers
- Old magazines
- Scissors
- Craft supplies

Once you've filled your pockets, head home and lay out your treasures on the table. You'll probably want to wash the dirt off and dry your rocks thoroughly before beginning the craft process. Next, take your shoe box and decorate it with construction paper, markers and other supplies. Get creative by cutting pictures of rocks and gems out of old magazines and gluing them on the inside and outside of the box. Have your son select his favorite rocks and paste them to the inside of the box using basic craft glue. Mark the date and location of each find, as any good geologist would do.

To top it off, cut a large "window" out of the lid of the shoe box and glue or tape a piece of plastic wrap over the hole (it's neater if you attach it to the inside of the lid). Now your son can show off his collection without having to remove the top of the box.

Make it harder: If you have a book that identifies rocks, or have access to the Internet, examine the rocks you've collected and try to identify them.

SAND ART

Boys love playing in the sand. They also love coloring. Combine these two passions with a colorful, sandy art project.

Set out four bowls on the table and pour about a cup of sand into each. Let your son add two or three drops of food coloring to each bowl and stir until well mixed. Pour and spread each bowl of sand onto a separate cookie sheet (so the different colors don't mix) and pop the sheets into the oven. Dry at 350°F for about 12 minutes. Remove the sheets and allow sand to cool for a few minutes.

Now the creativity begins. Have your son spread some glue on a piece of construction paper. It works best if he tries to make a design such as a big spiral or polka dots. Let him choose one of the colors of sand and sprinkle it on. Make sure he uses enough sand to thoroughly cover the

Materials Needed
- Sand
- Food coloring
- Glue
- Construction paper
- 4 bowls
- 4 spoons
- 4 cookie sheets

glue. Then, lift up the paper and pour off the excess sand. Make a new glue pattern and choose another color. Repeat the process until he has a colorful, sandy design. Let it dry and tack it to the fridge or hang it up in his room.

Make it harder: If your son is particularly creative, have him try sand bottle art, using the same colored sand. All he needs to do is pour the sand into a small empty bottle, one color at a time. Encourage him to experiment by tipping the bottle as he pours the sand, or by mixing the different colors before pouring them.

(49)

FROM ANOTHER GENERATION

Unless your parents live nearby, it's unlikely that your son gets to spend much time with senior citizens. And while it may not seem like a fun-filled activity to your son, he'll be quite surprised to learn just how interesting older people can be.

If you have a neighbor or acquaintance who is a senior citizen, ask them if it might be alright if you drop by with your son. Otherwise, call a nursing home or retirement center in your area and you'll likely be directed to the volunteer coordinator who will be more than happy to have you stop by for a visit.

It's a good idea to explain to your son why getting to know someone from an older generation is important. They have plenty of stories to tell and experiences to draw from. And most people in retirement homes don't get many visitors, so spending time with them is a treat. Once your son gets the idea, pack a few books and head out the door.

When you arrive, be sure your son introduces himself. To make everyone feel more comfortable, ask your son to read from one of the books he brought, or suggest that he ask the person you are visiting to read a few pages aloud. Then, initiate conversation about your son's life, encouraging him to recount adventures he has had lately. Many older people love hearing about children's escapades, as it brings them back to when they

were young. It's likely the person you are visiting will have a few stories to share about the past.

Don't overstay your welcome. A 30-minute visit is usually enough. And while you and your son brightened someone's day, your son got to meet and learn a little about an older person. Did he love it? Continue your visits on a regular basis. You'll be surprised how quickly a mutually beneficial relationship springs up.

(50)

SOCK PUPPETS

Ever get frustrated because your drawer is filled with mismatched socks? Put them to good use by making a family of sock puppets. Your son will enjoy creating them almost as much as he will love putting on puppet shows when they're ready.

Collect your socks, supplies and find a cozy place to sit. Get down to business by putting a sock on your son's hand like a mitten. Have him make a fist. With a pen, mark off where the eyes, nose and mouth should go on the puppet. Then, remove the sock and start decorating.

Materials Needed
- Socks
- Markers
- Yarn
- Cotton balls
- Buttons
- Bottle caps
- Thread
- Needle

Cotton balls, buttons or bottle caps work well as noses. Yarn, scraps of faux fur or a piece of shaggy carpet make good hair. Cut eyes out of magazines and glue them to the puppet's head. Or cut out some felt circles and sew them on. You can draw on the mouth, or use thin pieces of yarn to make lips. Encourage your son to add ears, a mustache, freckles and anything else he can think of to make his puppet complete.

Once the puppet family is ready, help your son create a play. Act out a favorite bedtime story or pretend the puppets represent his family or friends. Put on a show for other family members and make sure your son (as well as the puppets) take a big bow at the end!

Make it harder: Help your son build a puppet theater out of a large cardboard box. Cut it open along the back so it can unfold, then cut a large square out of the front for the "stage." Your son can hide under the hole and put the puppets above his head.

EASY PUZZLE

The only thing more exciting than solving a puzzle is solving a puzzle that you created! Start by laying six tongue depressors out on a flat surface. Line them up in a row with the edges touching. Tape them to the table by cutting two long pieces of tape and placing them over the tips of the depressors (both top and bottom).

Step two involves your son drawing a picture on these sticks. Use vibrant colors and make sure parts of the image overlap from one depressor to the next. All six sticks should have some art on them. Then, remove the tape and shuffle the tongue depressors around. His puzzle is ready.

Materials Needed

- Tape
- Markers
- Six tongue depressors (or cardboard or paper cut into thin strips)

Double the challenge by drawing on both sides. Or, draw on a piece of paper and then cut it into a variety of shapes when your son is done. Putting the odd shapes back together is harder than figuring out how the tongue depressor sticks fit together.

Make it easier: Number your sticks one through six,

mix them up and ask your son to re-arrange them into the proper order.

(52)

VACATION SCRAPBOOK

Preserve your vacation memories by building a scrapbook with mementos of your trip. More than just photographs, a vacation scrapbook is filled with tidbits detailing where you went, what you saw and what activities you participated in.

Before you head off on your trip, discuss the scrapbook idea with your son. Plan to collect items along the way that will go in the scrapbook such as postcards, ticket stubs, candy wrappers, napkins, business cards, brochures, maps and receipts. Just about any small item that can lie flat will do.

When you return home, pile your collection on the table. Try to pair items with the corresponding photograph. If you took a train, for example, put the photograph of your son standing in front of the train next to the ticket stub from the train. With

Materials Needed

• Miscellaneous items picked up on vacation
• Photos
• "Magnetic" photo album
• Markers
• Construction paper

construction paper and markers add fancy decorations to your scrapbook. An easy trick is to include the day of your trip and the location you were at that day (Day 1-Beach) on every page. Cut out maps and use a highlighter to designate the routes you traveled.

Now, open the "magnetic" pages and have your son arrange the items creatively. Laying things out chronologically makes it easier when it comes to telling people about your trip. All your son has to do is explain what each item on each page means.

Make it harder: Have your son write captions or add humorous comments in "balloons" coming from the mouths of the people in the photos.

READ-A-THON

The next time you and your son are faced with a rainy afternoon, host a read-a-thon instead of turning on the tube. Send your son on a hunt for ten of his favorite books while you prepare some snacks. Meet in the family room or other cozy corner and hunker down for an afternoon of reading.

Materials Needed

• Lots of good books
• Snacks

Explain to your son that there are four parts to the read-a-thon; reading aloud, listening, retelling and silent reading. If your son can read, take turns reading aloud. This activity goes hand in hand with listening carefully. Once you finish a book, ask your son to summarize the story. It's a great way to see if he comprehends what he hears. You can also initiate discussion by asking him which characters he liked or disliked, what would happen if there were a different ending and other such open-ended questions.

Silent reading is the fourth activity that can be done on its own or interspersed with the other parts of the read-a-thon. If he's too young to read by himself, help him sound out the words or let him tell his own story about the illustrations. Keep the snacks handy and be sure to encourage your son throughout the process. Pretty soon you'll have a bookworm on your hands.

Make it harder: Have your son write a brief report about each book.

SUPER BUBBLES

Super-size your bubble-blowing fun with things you have around the house; coat hangers, dish soap and a cookie sheet.

Gather your supplies and head outdoors. Dilute your dish soap with water (about half and half) or use bubble liquid from your local toy store. Then, pour the solution into the cookie sheet so it forms a shallow layer at the bottom. Untwist a coat hanger until it is one long piece of wire and then make a big loop out of it. Have your son submerge the hanger in the soap and carefully lift it out. There should be a film of soap across the entire loop.

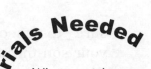

Materials Needed

• Wire coat hangers
• Dish soap
• Cookie sheet

Encourage your son to wave it through the air and watch a gigantic bubble form. Or, spin it around and around and watch a stream of bubbles shoot out.

With your spare hangers, try some variations. Twist the wire into three or four smaller loops to create a shower of bubbles. Or try making the wire into a square or triangular shape and see what results. Another fun

trick with super bubbles is catching a bubble within a bubble. Accomplish this by blowing a big bubble, then catching it with the wire ring. Gently blow on the bottom of it, forcing another bubble to appear within the first bubble!

This activity is a great precursor to bath time since your son will be in the bubble mood already!

BOY BOX

D oes your son leave his toys everywhere? Help him build a special box to store his treasures and your son will be eager to put them away when he's finished playing.

A successful Boy Box should be fairly large; about the size of a night stand. The wood doesn't have to be fancy—left over pieces from other projects are fine. Design the box on paper before you start cutting. Encourage your son to contribute ideas about how he'd like it to look. Unless you are a master carpenter, keep the design simple. Include some shelves to break up the space in the box and consider putting the door on the front—like a refrigerator—for easy access.

- Scrap wood
- Nails
- Screws
- Hinges
- Hammer
- Screwdriver
- Paint
- Markers
- Stickers
- Stencil

Now start putting the pieces together. Have your son help with the measuring and holding parts together as you attach them. Teach him the old axiom: Measure twice, cut once. A simple design should take less than an hour to complete. When it's done, it's your son's turn to paint the box and decorate it with markers, stickers, pictures or use a stencil to create a pattern. Let it dry and then help him stash his treasures inside.

Make it harder: A more elaborate design will enhance the challenge. Additions such as a latch on the door and secret spaces inside make the box even more special.

Make it easier: If a wooden box is too much for your son, make it out of a cardboard shoe box instead.

SHADOW GAMES

Is your son enthralled with shadows on his wall? Turn his fixation into a creative activity by hosting your own shadow puppet theater. It is a simple, fun way to spend an afternoon.

The most basic shadow puppets are those that you can create with your hands. If you want to take it a step further, however, gather some craft supplies and make a variety of puppets. Start by drawing some shapes on a thin piece of cardboard. If you aren't comfortable drawing free hand, trace around animal cookie cutters for the general shape of bears, birds, moose and any other animal you want to include in the show. Then, cut them out and attach pipe cleaner antlers, antennae and legs. Use pipe cleaners and tissue paper to make butterfly wings. Pieces of string make good tails. A few twists of a pipe cleaner, some glue and a little string make fun people with hair.

Plenty of household items such as spice jar lids, mesh bags, brooms and sponges make interesting shadows.

Materials Needed

- White sheet
- Lamp
- Thin cardboard
- Sticks
- Glue
- Hole punch
- Pipe cleaners
- String
- Tissue paper
- Cookie cutters
- Pen
- Scissors

Funky shapes and designs compliment your collection of animal and people puppets. Once you've finished creating, make sure each "puppet" has a stick or string attached to it so you can manipulate it without your hand being in the scene. Then, put together the theater by suspending a white sheet across a doorway or other convenient spot. Place a lamp (with the shade off) about eight feet from the sheet. Assemble some chairs on the other side of the sheet and send your son off to find an audience.

When everyone is seated, begin the show. Move, wiggle or dance your puppets between the sheet and the lamp. Everyone will be amazed at the results. If your son is younger, he might like a turn watching the show from the audience's perspective. Or, let him run the show and enjoy his creativity with the other audience members.

Make it harder: Make trees, houses, cars and other familiar items and have your son tell a story about the puppets he created.

(57)

CANDLE TRICKS

Most boys are very interested in pyro-technics, even if they are aware that playing with fire can be dangerous. In certain controlled situations, learning about the properties of fire is useful and amusing. For some fiery fun, try this scientific experiment.

Begin by explaining that air is made up of oxygen and nitrogen. People need air to breathe and fire needs it for food. Without air, fire could not exist. To put a fire out, you need to remove the air that is using as fuel. Once your son

Materials Needed

- Small candle
- Matches
- 3 different sized clear glasses
- Saucer
- Water
- Food coloring
- Watch

understands the basic way in which fire functions, move on to the demonstration.

Set your candle on the table and light it. Have your son carefully place the medium-sized glass over the candle. Using a watch, time how long it takes for the candle to extinguish. Explain that the flame will burn as long as there is oxygen in the glass. Once the candle uses up the oxygen, however, the flame will go out. Repeat this experiment with the larger glass. See if he can tell you why the candle burns longer the second time around.

For the second experiment, add a little food coloring to some water and pour a small amount of liquid into the bottom of a saucer. Light the candle and put it in the saucer. Place one of the glasses on top of the candle. Watch as the liquid gets sucked up into the glass as the fire starts to burn out. Ask your son if he can tell you why the water gets sucked up into the glass. Did he figure out that the liquid fills the space that the oxygen left when it was consumed by the flame?

DIRECTOR FOR A DAY

These days, making a home movie is a snap. So, help your son get in on the action by encouraging him to play director for a day. Whether you have a video camera that can hook up to your computer or an older model that records on VHS, teach your son the basics about how to use it. Then it's lights, camera and action!

Suggest that your son map out a basic storyline for his movie, whether it's about his stuffed animals, your family or his friends. Explain that all movie directors have a script to work with before they start filming. And while he probably doesn't need to write out every line, it's a good idea if his film has at least a little focus. Then, get to work.

Materials Needed

- Video camera
- Cardboard or construction paper
- Markers

If you are going to use a movie editing program to add music and credits later on, start collecting footage. If you'd rather keep it simple, make a few signs with construction paper that say, "The End" and "Credits." Pick a title and write that on a piece of paper too. Let your son do the taping himself with your guidance here and there if he needs it. Be ready in case your son gets frustrated with the way things are going. Often "actors" don't do all the things they are supposed to. Explain to your son that directors need to be very patient.

Once the production is wrapped up, gather the family, pop some popcorn, sit back and enjoy the show!

(59)

LOVE PILLS

There will come a time when your son is going to be apart from loved ones—Mom traveling for business, an older sibling going to summer camp or a favorite uncle moving to a new city. To ease the pain of loneliness for both parties, suggest that your son make a batch of Love Pills. These pills can even be made up in anticipation of routine separations such as your son attending kindergarten.

Pick up empty gelatin capsules at your local pharmacy. Set them out on the table and cut about 20 strips of paper approximately 1/4 of an inch wide by an inch long. With markers, crayons or pencils, help your son write a loving message on each strip of paper. They

Materials Needed

• Empty gelatin capsules
• Pen
• Paper
• Bottle

can be simple—"I miss you!"—or personal—"You are the best cook in the world!" If he can't write yet, let him dictate his messages to you then have him decorate the strips with crayons or markers.

Carefully roll up the strips as tightly as you can. Open the capsules, slip one strip into each and then replace the caps. Find an empty prescription drug bottle, rinse it out and remove the label (which should come off easily under warm water). Suggest that your son design his own label with the words "Love Pills" on it. Encourage him to write a prescription on the label such as "Take one daily or as needed when lonely."

Now put the pills into the bottle, recap it and wrap it up to give as a gift.

PERSONAL PLACEMATS

Setting the table is a task most kids can handle on their own, albeit grudgingly. Turn the chore into a fun-filled activity by encouraging your son to make personalized placemats for everyone in the family.

If your son is really young, start by showing him where the silverware and dishes go in a place setting. Next, ask him to draw them on an 8.5-inch x 11-inch piece of paper to remind when he's setting the table. Decorating this "placemat" is the best part of the activity. Help him make each one special by encouraging him to draw something personal. If his sister likes baseball, for example, he can color bats and balls on her mat. Writing each person's name is also a great idea.

You can do this on special occasions such as birthdays or holidays, but ordinary meals work too. Make it more complicated by decorating napkin holders (they can easily be made by stapling a strip of construction paper into a circle) and creating place markers. If your son cooks up something really special, have it laminated and use it over and over. This is one chore he'll look forward to!

Materials Needed

- Construction paper
- Markers
- Crayons

SHOPPING ALPHABET

Is your son just learning his ABCs? Play the shopping alphabet game to help him hone his skills and sharpen his mind.

Think of an item at a grocery store that starts with the letter A. Assume, for example, that you choose Apple. Say to your son, "I went to the market and bought something that starts with A." Your son then has to guess what it was that you bought. Once he guesses Apple, he continues the game by saying, "I went to the market and bought an apple and something that starts with a B." Now you try and guess what he bought. Then, you continue the game by saying, "I went to the market and bought an apple, bananas and something that starts with a C." The game progresses until you've gone through the whole alphabet. You'll be amazed at how good your son's memory is and he'll enjoy exercising it.

To add variety to the game, change the type of store. Instead of the market, pretend you went to the hardware or department store. Or, change the venue altogether by visiting the beach, the garage or your son's bedroom.

Make it harder: In addition to memorizing the list of

things purchased, keep a running count of the items purchased. For example, buy three apples, two peaches and seven cans of soup, for a total of 12 items.

THERMOMETER

C reate a handy household item and perform an interesting science experiment all the same time by making a thermometer.

Begin by laying out your materials. Next, have your son pour equal amounts of water and rubbing alcohol into the bottle until it is 1/3 full (you may want to use a measuring cup). Add a few drops of food coloring, seal the lid and shake it up. Remove the cap and insert a straw into the bottle. Have your son hold the straw so it hangs straight down the middle of the bottle, just short of touching the bottom. Using the clay, plug the bottle top closed (this will also hold the straw in place).

Put the bottle into your son's hands and watch what happens to the liquid. As the liquid warms, it will slowly begin to rise up the straw, just like a real ther-

Materials Needed

- Small plastic bottle
- Straw
- Water
- Rubbing alcohol
- Food coloring
- Modeling clay

mometer. Ask your son if he knows what happens to the molecules as they heat up. Explain the science behind it: When liquids are warmed, the molecules begin to move faster and faster, causing them to spread farther apart. This makes the liquid expand. As the liquid in the bottle expands, the only place for it to go is up the straw. (Since the top of the bottle was sealed, the air pressure within the bottle prevented the liquid from just rising in the bottle itself.)

This experiment has a long life because your son can observe the thermometer in the different environments; sun, shade, wind, indoors and out.

(63)

WOODSHOP BOAT

Watching Dad build something in his workshop is always a thrill for little boys. From hammers to nails to saws, tykes are fascinated with tools. Let your son participate by helping him build a wooden boat. As long as you provide proper supervision and instruction, you should have no trouble creating this tub-worthy vessel.

Materials Needed

- Scrap wood
- Screws
- Nails
- Screwdriver
- Hammer
- Saw

Start by teaching your son how to use basic tools; a saw, screwdriver and hammer. (It's a good idea to keep your power tools out of reach.) Explain how tools can be dangerous but that if your son is careful, all will go well. If you have a miter box, have your son use that. Not only does it facilitate a nice straight cut, but it also holds the saw steady. You might want to start the cut yourself and let your son finish the job.

The main part of this construction is the hull. Find any narrow, thin chunk of scrap wood and together with your son, saw one end into a point (forming the bow of the boat). Next, saw another piece of wood into a square for the cabin. Before you attach it to the boat, however, nail a long, skinny piece of wood to the back of the cabin for a mast. This job will teach your son how to use a hammer. Then, with a screwdriver and screw, attach the cabin to the boat.

It is possible to drive a wood screw into soft wood without a drill. Just wipe the screw on a bar of soap to lubricate it. With a few light taps of the hammer, anchor your screw into the wood. Insert the screwdriver and give it a few twists to get it started. Let your son drive it the rest of the way.

Now your boat is ready to be decorated. Paint the hull or make a sail out of an old sheet. Then, set your boat afloat in the bathtub or local pond.

(64)

BACKYARD CAMPOUT

For a quintessential father-son experience, plan a campout in your backyard. This relatively simple activity provides hours of entertainment and bonding time for you and your tyke.

Before dark, scout out the area where you want to set up camp. If you don't have a backyard, contact your

Materials Needed
• Sleeping bags
• Pup tent
• Pillows
• Deck of cards
• Snacks
• Flashlights

municipality to see if you can camp in a nearby park overnight. Then pitch your tent together, far enough from the house to make it feel as though you are actually in the wilderness. Arrange your sleeping bags and put the flashlights in a convenient location.

Before bedtime, take a nature hike in your backyard or through your neighborhood. Sit outside the tent and gaze up at the stars. When your son's bedtime nears, climb into the tent and turn on the flashlights. Munch on a snack while you tell campfire stories or play a hand of cards. Click off the lights and listen to the sounds of the night before drifting off to sleep.

In the morning, race inside for a relaxing shower. Sit down to a hot breakfast and share memories of your exciting adventure.

Make it harder: A campfire with toasted marsh-mallows makes a backyard campout more lavish. Make sure your son knows basic fire safety, and that your municipality allows ground fires, before lighting the logs.

Make it easier: Camping out in the living room can be a comfortable, warm, dry substitute to backyard camp-ing, particularly for children who may be scared by unfamiliar night sounds.

RAINY DAY GAMES

Plenty of activities both indoors and out are perfect for a rainy day. If it's warm, don waterproof clothing, pack an umbrella and meet the storm head on. Playgrounds, zoos and other "sunny-day" adventures are guaranteed to be free of crowds when the skies are grey.

Or, you can make your own fun by splashing through puddles and sending twig boats sailing the streams formed by the pouring rain. Try diverting the flow of water by building a dam of pebbles and mud. Keep an eye out for worms forced above ground by the wetness. Your son will probably get a kick out of helping these wiggly creatures from the sidewalk or road to the grass.

If you'd rather stay dry, read books about thunderstorms and learn why lightening is dangerous. See if your son can figure out where rain comes from and why lakes and streams don't often overflow. Discuss how rain helps trees and plants stay alive. Have a warm bowl of soup and watch a movie. Before you know it, the sun will be shining!

SILLY POEMS

Want to foster a love for literature in your son? Start early by playing the Silly Poems game. Even youngsters with minimal vocabulary enjoy and benefit from a round or two of this amusing activity.

Start by cutting the paper into small strips, just big enough to hold one word. Next, divvy up the strips so each of you have ten. With a pen or pencil, write down one word on each scrap of paper. Any words will do, and the sillier the better. If your son is stumped, suggest he take a quick tour around the house for inspiration. To make things easier, include several verbs and nouns in your group of ten words. Next, fold each strip in half and add them all to a bowl or hat. Offer your son first pick of the words. Alternately select a piece of paper until you each have ten.

Here's the challenging part. You and your son now have to make poems from the ten words you have selected. The poem can be as few as one or as many as ten lines. The only rules in this game are that all ten words must be used and none

Materials Needed

• Blank paper
• Scissors
• Pen or pencil
• Bowl or hat

can be added. Once you've created a literary master-piece, take turns reading your poems to each other. Poetry is often about how words sound together, so reading them out loud is a good way to hear just how silly or creative your poem is.

If you come up with a doozy, paste the words to a piece of paper, decorate or illustrate it, and tack it up on the fridge. If neither of you is satisfied, put your words back into the mix and try again. You can add more words to make it more interesting, or have a race to see who can make a poem the fastest. However you chose to play, you and your son will definitely giggle over silly word combinations.

Make it harder: Increase the poem to 15 words, or set more restrictions, such as requiring two words per line. Or, allow the players to add extra words as needed, as long as they use the ten they pulled from the hat.

Make it easier: Son can't write? Draw simple pictures instead and use those to create a picture poem!

67

A REAL MEAL

The next time the cook in your household wants a break, suggest that your son prepare a family dinner rather than eating out. Making supper will help your son understand the time and effort that goes into preparing meals. It can also be loads of fun, as boys enjoy getting messy in and around the kitchen.

Although your son might want to create something lavish, suggest that the first time you attempt this activity you keep it simple. Let your son do most of the planning, from deciding on the ingredients to picking the dessert. Explain to your son that a balanced, healthy meal should include something from each of the food groups. Show him a food chart so he can visualize the different types of food he needs to include.

Materials Needed

• Ingredients for a meal

Once he's planned a menu (macaroni and cheese and a salad is a good start), decide which steps in the meal-making process your son can handle. Retrieving ingredients, pouring and mixing are obvious chores for a youngster and probably all he'll need to feel satisfied with his part.

Let him arrange the food decoratively on each plate

and if he wants, explain to your family why each food that he chose is important to keep them healthy and strong. If your son usually sets the table, give him a break this time around since he has helped prepare the meal. But make sure he realized that preparing dinner also includes putting all the ingredients away and storing the leftovers in the fridge.

Make it harder: Obviously, the more complicated the meal, the more of a challenge it will be. Still looking for ways to increase the challenge? Ask him to write out a fancy menu for each family member.

Make it easier: Little boys will feel they've contributed even if they're input is limited to choosing the meal or helping with a few ingredients.

PLANT A TREE

Want to give your son something that will survive long after he's grown out of his hockey cards, toy cars and stuffed animals? Consider planting a tree together. You'll be able

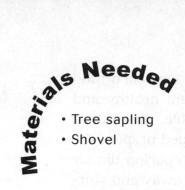
measure its growth alongside that of your son's for many years to come.

Start by choosing a location to plant your sapling. It needs to be out of the way so that it won't get accidentally trampled but it also needs adequate sunlight. Got a spot? The next step is to pick a sapling. It's much more satisfying to watch the rapid progress of a young sapling than the slow and steady growth of a bigger tree. Select a species based on your local climate, how much space there is in your yard and your son's personal taste. Most local greenhouses can recommend a type of tree that will be well suited to your environment.

The messy part of the job starts when you dig the hole for the sapling. Help your son shovel the hole deep enough so that the roots will hang freely when the bottom of the trunk is level with the top of the hole. Turn on the hose and run water into the hole until it's half full. Put the sapling in the hole so trunk starts at ground level. Have your son fill the hole up with the dirt, lightly packing it as he goes. When the hole is filled, the sapling should be able to stand on its own. Water again so the soil is thoroughly soaked and settles around the roots of the tree.

The key to survival for your sapling is water and protection. Your son should water the tree every day for the first two weeks and then every other day for a month

(longer if the weather is dry). Spray enough water so that it puddles up under tree. You should also consider erecting a little fence around the trunk so that other kids and creatures keep away from the delicate sapling.

Depending on the species and growing conditions, your tree can grow a foot or more in the first season, then sprout another couple of feet in the following year. Twenty years from now your son can return and sit under a towering tree and remember what fun it was to plant it with Dad!

A SHAVE A DAY

There's nothing that brings fathers and sons together better than a good shave. Shocked? Don't be. Boys love watching Dad lather on the shaving cream. So, the next time you catch him watching you trim your whiskers, invite him to join you!

First, run a washcloth under warm water and have your tyke hold the wet washcloth to his cheeks and chin. Ask him to hold out his hand while you squirt some shaving cream into it. Show him the proper way to apply shaving cream, making sure he covers his entire "beard" and avoids the eye area.

Materials Needed

• Shaving cream
• Warm washcloth
• Playing card

Then, hand him a playing card or some other item with a firm, dull edge. Demonstrate the correct manner in which to use a "razor" to wipe off the cream. Let him rinse the card off in water as needed. He should keep at it until his face is clean. Give him the wet washcloth again so he can wipe off any residue.

Show an appreciation for a job well done by rubbing your finger gently down his cheek and remarking on what a clean shave he's achieved. Then, head off to breakfast together.

MINI-GOLF

Enjoy golf? Get your son involved in a game of putt-putt by creating a miniature course in your house or yard. You'll both get a kick out of making tricky holes and then playing a round or two.

Half the fun of this activity is designing the course. Take a bit of extra time to come up with creative, challenging holes. Plot out your course and then build ramps, tunnels, buildings or other obstacles for the duffers to tackle. You can even pick a theme and design your obstacles accordingly; a castle and moat is an easy option.

Use materials you have lying around the house to make the holes and obstacles. A cardboard box with a semi-circular shape cut out of either side along the bottom makes a good building. Cut out the bottom of a coffee can and lay it on its side for a tunnel. Make ramps out of plywood or cardboard propped up with bricks or some of your son's blocks. Bowls buried in the ground and filled with liquid make good water hazards. To make the actual holes, dig

Materials Needed

- Golf balls and clubs (or an appropriate substitute)
- Garbage pail
- Recycling bin
- Cardboard boxes
- Coffee cans
- Bowls

a little dirt out of the ground and set a plastic cup into it. Or, if you're playing indoors, turn the cup over on its side. Toys, chairs, books and other household items also make challenging obstacles.

You can set a par for each hole, or just decide that the one who manages to sink the ball in fewer strokes wins, even it if it takes several tries. Then, pull out the clubs and away you go!

(71)

SECRET CODE

Encryption and coding has become a complex process now that we have entered the world of cyber-interactions. Get into the game by creating a secret code that only you and your son know how to "break." A special bond between the two of you will develop as you share harmless secrets.

There are dozens of simple codes you can use to communicate with your son. Once you choose your method of encryption, learning the system is the only part of this activity that is grueling. Once you've both mastered the art of writing in secret code, the message exchange can begin!

One code you can try is the Letter-Number Code. On

a strip of paper, write out the alphabet. Now add a number under each letter, starting with 1 under A, 2 under B and so on until each letter has a number associated with it. When you want to use this code, simply write a message using the corresponding numbers instead of letters (so if you wanted to write Hello, you would mark down 8-5-12-12-15). Include a dash between each number and a space between each word.

Another possibility is the Backward Code. To encrypt something using this code, write each word of your message backwards. For example, instead of writing the sentence "secret coding is fun" you would mark down "terces gnidoc si nuf." Any youngster that intercepts notes using this code will definitely be stumped.

Looking for something a little more challenging? Try using the Hidden Word Code. Start by writing out your message. Then, use each letter of the first word as the first letter of a word in a new, coded sentence. Say your original message is "You are special." Using the code, you could write: Young owl upset. Apples roll everywhere. Someone put Ed's chow in a lid. To crack this code, all your son has to do is put the first letter of every word together. Too complex? An easy variation of this code involves using each word of your secret message as the first word in a sentence. "You are special" could be transformed into "YOU need a bath. ARE you coming home? SPECIAL delivery for someone small." Anyone who doesn't know the key to unlocking this secret message will be at a loss to understand the nonsense sentences.

Tuck secret messages in your son's lunch, under his pillow or slip them onto his plate at dinner. He'll love decoding them and you'll enjoy watching his face light up when he solves the puzzle!

(72)

STORY CHAIN

Next time you and your son or other family members are sitting around looking bored, launch into a story. But instead of making the whole thing up yourself, take turns inventing the plot. Start a story off by reciting a few sentences, then turn to your son and ask "what happens next?" Encourage his creativity by finishing up your part with a cliffhanger.

These stories are usually nonsensical, taking wild twists every time someone new takes over the storytelling. If your son is stumped, help him along by asking leading questions such as "Did a dinosaur suddenly appear?" or "Did the lights go out?" Part of this activity's focus is being able to listen carefully to the person who is telling the segment before you so you'll be able to build on the action when your turn rolls around.

For kids who can write, transform this oral activity into something that will last by writing it down in a notebook. Start by writing an introduction and then let your son try his hand at adding twists to the plot. Leave it around so other family members can contribute as well. Pretty soon you'll have a literary masterpiece on your hands!

(73)

FACE PAINTING

Face painting is a big draw for kids. Unfortunately, it often involves waiting in long lines at a party or fair and the results can be less than spectacular. The next time your son wants to get creative, suggest that you paint his face right in your own home.

Start by washing his face and applying moisturizer or a light coat of petroleum jelly. It'll make the removal process much easier. Then, discuss what type of design he'd like. If he's a bit anxious, suggest something small on his cheek rather than a full face mask. Painting the logo of his favorite sports team is always a hit!

You don't have to be a great artist to create animal

faces such as cats, tigers or mice. Action heroes are also a common request, and as long as you know what they look like, it's a pretty simple feat to accomplish. Have your son look through books to find an example of the face he'd like. Working from a picture can often be helpful.

Once he's made a choice, don old clothes or a smock. Let him hold a mirror while you go to work. It's important to keep away from the eye area. Once you've finished your masterpiece, let your son try his hand at being an artist. He'll love the chance to paint a design on Dad's face.

Soap and water should wash away any paint residue when you want to return to your normal selves.

TWIRL PICTURES

Design and craft magic art with Twirl Pictures. They are not only fun to make, but also to play with once you have finished decorating them.

Start by folding a piece of construction paper into a rectangle about four inches tall and three inches wide. Now have your son draw half a picture on one side of the paper, such as an ice cream cone with no ice cream in it, a tree with no leaves, or a person with no hair. On the other side of the folded paper draw the missing part of the front picture, in roughly the spot it would go if you were to combine the front and back sides. Make sure each side of the picture is a different color. If your son has drawn an ice cream cone, for example, make the cone brown and color the scoop of ice cream pink.

Unfold the paper. Tape a pencil or other stick-like object to the back of the construction paper (on the opposite side to where the cone or tree is). Then re-fold the paper so the pencil is sandwiched in between your two drawings. Tape the sides together and make sure the pencil hangs down far enough so it looks like you have a cardboard popsicle on a stick.

Materials Needed

- Pencils
- Construction paper
- Crayons
- Markers
- Tape

Put the pencil between your palms. Show your son the front side (cone or tree) and then quickly roll the pencil between your hands so that picture flips back and forth so you see the cone and then the ice cream, the tree and then its branches. Magically, it will appear as though the ice cream is sitting on the cone and the branches attached to the tree.

Your son will be amazed by the optical illusion and he'll want to show it off to all his friends.

(75)

LEAFY FUN

Playing in the fall leaves is an awesome autumn activity. Join in the fun by building a leaf fort with your son.

Begin by raking the leaves on your lawn into a huge pile. There are two basic ways to construct a fort. The easiest way is to create a "nest" in the middle of the pile by digging a hole in the middle of your pile and pushing the leaves out towards the edges. This simple fort is perfect for tots.

For a more sophisticated version, find a big cardboard box (refrigerator boxes

Materials Needed

• Rakes
• Cardboard box

work well), lay it on its side and cover it with leaves. Leave one side (where the box opens) uncovered so you can get in and out of your leaf fort easily. If you happen to have two boxes, make two forts so you can each have one as your base camp.

You can also make a leaf slide or have a leaf fight. Try burying yourself or your son in the leaves to see what it feels like. End your day by each picking five of your favorite leaves and comparing colors and sizes.